# When Prosecutors Attack!

*OJ Simpson, Roderick Scott, George Zimmerman – Baseless Government Attacks and the Media That Lets It Happen*

Authored By

**Niles Mercado**

ISBN: 0615871453
ISBN-13: 978-0615871455

# DEDICATION

I dedicate this book to my Father who taught me reason, logic, impartiality, faith and how to be a man.

# CONTENTS

# ACKNOWLEDGMENTS

Cover Artist: **Ritchie Hamilton**
Editor: **Elliot I.K.**
Copy and Research Consultant: **P.I.K.**
Proof Reader: **J.M.K.**
Special Consultant: **Peter Fernando A.**

# SPECIAL THANKS

**Pat McKenna**, for taking the time to be interviewed for this book and providing key insights that aided in our investigation.

**William C. Thompson**, for granting us permission to quote extended passages from:
*DNA Evidence in the O.J. Simpson Trial, Colorado Law Review, 67 (4), 827-857 (1996)*

**Anonymous, Esq,** our legal consultant that has understandably decided to keep her identity hidden.

**Sundance**, the moniker used by one of our key anonymous researchers whose research and successful FOIA requests helped us heavily throughout the last chapter of this book and whose contribution came at a great personal cost to himself and his family.

And lastly… thanks to my **14-month old daughter** who sat peacefully on my lap during at least a quarter of the writing of this book.

# DISCLAIMERS

- Absolutely nothing in this volume is meant to constitute legal, financial, or medical advice nor are the opinions presented to be considered expert opinions.
- I am convinced that the three defendants we analyze are innocent. That said each particular detail is presented to the best of my knowledge and understanding. If you have any concrete proof that any detail in this volume is inaccurate **please email us** and we will correct it and publish an updated edition (nilesmercado@gmail.com).
- I have **deep respect for America's collective police force**. An officer saved my father's life when he was a child so I would not even be alive today without their service. However in this volume, while you will see that the Greece PD and Sanford PD acted honorably for the most part, the unfortunate truth is that **several LAPD officers did not act with honor** and brought shame on their department.
- **No prosecutors were hurt** in the writing, editing and publishing of this volume. *Seriously though, despite the evidence and analysis presented in this volume, the Author has deep respect for all those that seek to enforce the law fairly and without consideration to the advancement of their own careers, politics and personal gain.*
- Absolutely no portion of this book was written in a Starbucks.

# PUBLISHERS NOTE

This work by Niles Mercado I believe is groundbreaking in many ways. His writing is bold, bright, and enjoyable; it jumps right off the page as if each chapter is an intense conversation he is having with you right there in your living room.

Before releasing this flagship title, Level Press has focused on niche titles, everything from technical manuals to targeted aficionado literature. With the release of "**When Prosecutors Attack**" we have what is sure to be our first broadly appealing bestseller.

Any readers coming to this volume thinking they are going to be reading a dry legal treatise **are in for an incredibly enjoyable treat**.

Making use of vividly bold language, untraditional formatting, tables, liberal use of photos, **professionally crafted flowcharts**, and other **modern mechanisms** for presenting concepts and data we have put together a title that is easy and **fun to absorb** while at the same time being **densely informative**.

Few traditional publishers have adjusted to the seismic shift the modern reader has undergone; readers that are looking for enjoyable and informative titles that can deliver densely informative material in an intensely fun manner. The modern reader, me included, picks up quickly when they feel that a writer is **FILLING UP** space just to pad the size of a particular chapter for some misguided attempt at overall symmetry or to reach an artificially higher page count.

At Level Press we demand that our Authors are honest about their content and insist that they **remove anything that feels like filler** and are constantly asking them if part of what they are trying to explain **could be *shown* rather than *told*** and if that would **enrich the end users experience** (sort of the adults version of "Show and Don't Tell" when appropriate) and then assist them in structuring their data in a manner that is immediately discernible to the modern reader.

We know you will enjoy absorbing "**When Prosecutors Attack**", I certainly enjoyed reading its first submission and enjoyed the final cut even more as I am sure you will now. We also choose Authors that like to interact with their readers and who thrive off of that type of feedback.

We are also EAGER to hear from you so please drop me a line when you get a chance. Enjoy this fantastic read and be sure to pass the pleasure along to your friends and family so all can get to enjoy this unique literary experience!

Publisher and Founder,
Level Press

Jo RoK

(Pronounced ROCK)
levelproperty@gmail.com

**"After a violent crime, both the damaged victim and society seek the equilibrium of prosecution, as relentlessly as ice will melt"**

**– Barry Scheck and Peter Neufeld**
**(As Quoted from "Actual Innocence")**

# WHEN PROSECUTORS ATTACK!

Life on Earth is occasionally disrupted by inexplicable attacks by an ominous and sometimes deadly force. Most of us aren't directly affected but we look on in shock and awe while our fellow citizens are targeted and their lives are destroyed.

These alien-like attackers often destroy their targets, but what is even more disconcerting are the family members that have to see their father, son or brother decimated and can do nothing about it.

To add insult to injury the mainstream media doesn't expose these attacks and awaken the citizenry at large to these imperial advances. Instead they cheer it on and sit back and enjoy the ratings. It is almost as if they have something to gain by making friends with these terrestrial occupiers.

Unfortunately I am not describing some fictional Sci-Fi scenario (*excuse redundancy*) but I am talking about:

**WHEN PROSECUTORS ATTACK!**

To be clear I am **not here to cast aspersions on prosecutors in general** (as the law needs to be enforced as we all know) but rather to point out several cases **When Prosecutors Attack**. My own experience being arrested (for the gross offense of driving with a suspended license that was suspended for an **unpaid parking ticket**) changed my perspective to actually view prosecutors and police more favorably than I had viewed them beforehand. Growing up watching a copious array of courtroom dramas led me to think that defendants were often, if not usually, innocent. Now most shows favor the police and prosecution but in the 1990's and shortly thereafter you had TV shows like "The Practice" and "Boston Legal" that glorified the defense. After my arrest and 25-hour incarceration I came to realize two important facts that changed my perspective significantly.

**First**, that most people that get arrested should get arrested because they have indeed committed a crime. Why do I say this? Well I was held in "the Tombs" in NYC after my arrest and in a jail cell overnight with about 30 other men. **Down to a person they all admitted their guilt** freely and openly. While I think arresting someone for an unpaid parking ticket is outrageous, even I should have been there according to the law. If they readily admitted their guilt I have no reason to question it. Also while this certainly is not a scientific survey by any means, I think the fact that out of 31 detainees not one tried to claim innocence during our idle conversations is significant and it starts to be clear why people tend to think that those arrested and prosecuted are probably guilty.

**Secondly,** however, one thing that became clear is that across the board charges were also trumped up a bit. In theory, it could be that detainees would be completely candid about their guilt but then duplicitous about all the charges when they had nothing to gain from this deception-candor combo – it is much more likely that adding some extra charges is a common practice perhaps used so that the prosecutor can get the perpetrator to plea to the crimes of which they are actually guilty (this explanation may seem a little too easy or naïve to some but I am trying to give prosecutors the benefit of the doubt before we get into some cases of obvious abuse).

With all that said my two realizations stated above are **completely irrelevant** when evaluating each individual case. It appears that the fact that most people arrested are guilty has started to snowball on itself as people are becoming more and more trusting of the government with each passing case.

To put this in terms of cold hard numbers the **conviction rate** (*total amount of convictions divided by the total number of prosecutions*) in 1972 was **an arguably healthy 75%** - three out of every four cases brought to a jury and judge ended in a conviction. By 1992, just twenty short years of increased media consumption later, the conviction rate had soared to 85%, a ten point seismic shift. Has this trend of increasing confidence in the government's prosecutions abated since the early 1990's? Hardly! In fact, as of 2011 the US Department of Justice reported a **sobering 93%** conviction rate!

Less than seven out of **100** (one hundred) cases are won by the defense. This could mean that the government has just shifted away from prosecuting the innocent. It could mean prosecutors have just improved in their legal skills at a time when defense attorneys simultaneously are turning into bumbling and fumbling laughing stocks. However these are very unlikely scenarios. It is much more likely that more and more people are **losing the ability to think critically**; that more and more people are short circuiting their thought process: *"Well, most people arrested are guilty so unless the defense can* ***prove*** *otherwise I'm going to think they are guilty"* when **it is of course the "people's burden" to prove guilt.**

Like I said, even I believe that most people arrested are guilty of something but that vague, seemingly true, statement is really quite mentally lazy and useless when brought into any particular examination. I for one find it **deeply unsettling** to see such an increase in convictions. Turning the state on your fellowman should be reserved for **serious offenses with solid evidence** free of any reasonable doubt. I guess I should be glad that the US conviction rate isn't as high as it is in Japan where over 99% are convicted! Could you imagine being on trial in a country like that? In Japan's defense they say they have systematically underfunded their prosecutors and courts so that only the overly obvious cases are ever brought to trial. The veracity of that claim is way beyond my purview so I will just say that I hope that it is true and we can get back to this country. By now, though, we likely agree that **there should be no presumption of guilt** for defendants in general and that we can examine the three main cases of this book without such a presumption.

On that point I should mention that during the OJ Simpson trial the **media constantly complained** that the jury presumed his innocence because of his acting and athletic stardom. However, in the

US defendants are **supposed** to be "presumed innocent until proven guilty" so really we should be glad that OJ was presumed innocent and we should be lamenting that normal defendants do not get that benefit. In a so-called free society to have the media wining about a defendant not having a presumption of guilt is nothing short of staggering.

Before moving on though let's acknowledge that there is a reason why most cases are never heard of by most of us. When someone holds up a convenience store, shoots the clerk, gets caught by the police on the way out and there are security videos and live witnesses we don't really hear about that case. Most cases are fairly open and shut so there is no reason for media attention. If we do see it in the news it's a passing story and usually reported at the local or regional level.

The media picks up stories for one of two reasons (and sometimes both), the first reason being if the case has some mystery and complexity to it that leave the audience guessing which makes each development in the case interesting. When the evidence is clear cut and a conviction is obvious the case loses interest by most people. The second reason the media **picks up stories is if they meet some political template** that they want to drive home. This shows the uglier side of the media's role in society. The media (and arguably the political system at large) thrives on dividing people along racial, economic, political and gender-based lines. So we see lots of Black vs. White, Police vs. Minority, Rich vs. Poor, Man vs. Woman, gun owner vs. anti-gun advocates, and it goes on and on.

In this book I do not seek to jump on the bandwagon and further the divide. Instead it is my earnest hope that this work will serve to be conciliatory, to in **some small way ease the divide** between Black and White, Rich and Poor, Citizen and Police, Man and Woman, etc. I will get into this more in the next chapter but for now let me just say that the cases I decided to cover in this volume were chosen carefully because they run the gambit in terms of rich, poor, black, white, honorable law enforcement and corrupt police.

However, the common denominators in the cases we will cover will be that the defendants were innocent of the crimes they were charged with and the prosecutors were unjustly on the attack.

It is nearly impossible that you will agree with me completely at the outset of this discussion. **Usually the people that think** OJ Simpson is innocent are the same people that think George Zimmermann is guilty (and vice versa). Chances are you haven't even heard about Roderick

Scott but it's similarity to the Zimmermann case just could not be ignored.

All I ask is that you keep an open mind and try and put your initial emotional reaction to what you are reading aside. If you can do that then we can discuss these matters rationally. You may not agree with everything in this volume but we don't *have to* agree on everything to see value in each other's viewpoints, do we?

In fact I will be quoting from books and documentaries that I don't necessarily agree with in whole so please don't take a simple quote from a work as an endorsement by me of it in its entirety.

For example, one groundbreaking work on the OJ Simpson case was a documentary called "Serpent's Rising" that contains several strong eye-opening points. There is also a small segment in the film that I find mildly anti-Semitic that I immediately dismissed as irrelevant and unfortunate. Does that mean that I need to reject everything they have to say because one detail in their presentation offends my intelligence and sense of decency (not to mention ethnic background)? Certainly not! If you think about it, the network news programs could hardly live up to that standard and as the Good Book states "in the abundance of words there is transgression".

So in that spirit I hope you will evaluate each of the points presented in this book separately and without prejudice. I will lay out the information the only way I know how and that is frankly and bluntly. It is my hope that you are comfortable enough with your own viewpoint to not be threatened by a differing view and that you continue reading until the end. When you finish reading this I also sincerely hope to hear from you and will try to answer any email that appears to be written by someone that actually took the time to read this book (nilesmercado@gmail.com).

In actuality I have very high expectations of my readers. The fact that you have picked up this volume is evidence that you are an inquisitive, interested, likely open minded and literate individual. Please do not take for granted your ability and inclination to think critically because it is not that prevalent today. In my upcoming eBook **"Zombie Thinkers: The Dumification of Emuriqa"** I walk through why critical thinking is so rare today which helps explain why the general public isn't up in arms **When Prosecutors Attack!**

But right now, before we can really dig into these cases we should probably just **address the** **giant elephant** in the room since it is kind of hard to focus on anything else until we do.

# **RACE**: THE ELEPHANT IN THE ROOM

We often use expressions repeatedly without taking a moment to remember where they come from. I always like analogies involving animals because they are so vivid and plus it gives us a moment in our modern lives to visualize something in nature. The **elephant** in the room is a good example of this. If you are in doors at this moment imagine if there was a **giant elephant** in the room you are in. Now imagine that someone is trying to carry on a conversation with you but is making no reference to the **elephant**. Clearly you are not going to be able to focus on what they are saying until they at least make reference to it.

If you can't get the **elephant** out of the room then the next best thing is to just address it, talk about it so you both know where you stand and see if you can gain some common ground on how to deal with the large grey mammal.

Well, when it comes to the subject of race we are obviously not going to "get it out of the room" so we might as well discuss it briefly. Let me start by saying that in general I am so tired of hearing about and having to talk about race. I mean race is such an arbitrary thing to be dominating our perception of the world. I had a very unique upbringing in that the faith I was brought up in is one of the few Christian denominations that has integrated worship. I didn't really think this was anything remarkable growing up, to me it was just normal, but as I got older I came to realize that weekly worship is actually **the most segregated activity** in American life. So work, schooling, recreation, and even dating is less segregated in this country than worship.

If you are curious I am of mostly Latin background, my mother is Puerto Rican and my father's family was made up of Sephardic Jews from Spain and Turkey (before converting to Christianity in the 1950's). While we lived in a mostly white neighborhood the congregation we attended was about a quarter black and the other three quarters were a mix of every other possibility you could think of (Asian, Latin, European-Whites, ethnically Jewish converts, etc.) and since my family was very religious the congregation was really at the center of our lives growing up and thus shaped my impressions of other races.

Since all the men would dress in suits and ties and the woman would wear formal dresses I grew up with deep respect for all races. Also, in our denomination we were all trained in public speaking so everyone for the most part was very articulate and well spoken. I was exposed to family heads of every race and looked up to the older men who took the lead in the congregation who were of every race. When our family would entertain there was usually a mix of backgrounds but to be honest it really wasn't something we thought too much about. Our relationships were based on our common faith so race was hardly brought up as an important subject.

Of course I was also exposed to television where these artificial racial roles are constantly forced down everyone's throat. To be honest until I got older I thought that no one really bought into these racial roles or took the media's race perception seriously. Of course as I got older I came to realize that race identification (especially self-identity) often runs very deep with people. My elementary school was mostly white and then when I got to middle-school which was about 20% black I started to hear race discussed as a significant issue (usually in the context of racial slants like "cracker" or on the flipside occasionally the N-word).

It all seemed so silly to me and made me proud of my upbringing. However, since then I've been very keenly aware of when race is brought up in a disparaging manner. To be honest I've never really seen someone's race hold them back or close an opportunity occupationally. This could be because the field I chose to pursue; at a young age I started working in the software development field which (especially during the tech boom when developers were desperately sought after) cared only about qualifications.

When I managed my own professional services team and was responsible for hiring I remember that race could not have been further from my mind. I would say that I only care about three questions: 1) do you have the technical know-how? 2) Do you have a good work ethic and attitude and 3) when can you start?

That said I would never make the ridiculous claim that I am "color blind". I don't know who coined this term but unless you are actually blind it is impossible not to notice someone's racial background when you meet them. The human retina (or your eye) can transmit to your brain roughly 10 million bits of information every single second. So when you meet someone you aren't blind to any aspect of their appearance. Within a short second your brain has information on their height, gender, manner, dress (or lack thereof) and yes race (let alone what the other senses are telling your brain).

So we have a little common ground – yes people see someone's race as part of them but no we should not be using race to judge our fellow man. I just wanted to make that clear because in this volume I am really forced to address racial issues but I wanted you to know where I stood and a little about me so you can see where I am coming from.

## Media Creates the Racism It Reports

But when it comes to the mainstream media they regularly frame news stories in a racial context. In the 1990's my whole family was shocked at how race was used by the media in the OJ Simpson trial. With all of the heavy-handed politically correct television programming in that decade we were astonished at how nearly all the pundits framed the OJ Simpson acquittal in racial terms by blaming a "black jury" for his acquittal. Beyond being racist this was just mentally lazy. Just watch the interviews with the Jurors and you see that these were intelligent coherent individuals who had no gripe with the police in general terms. Also, we wanted to scream at the television that it was not a "black" but had three white jurors. Even so, the whole issue of the jury's race was completely irrelevant since even all-black juries regularly convict blacks of murder and all sorts of other crimes. I mean no sane human being wants murderers walking around in their communities.

Many would simply brand the media's reaction to the OJ Simpson verdict as racist (if they understood from the facts of the case that the verdict was correct) but I think what we saw was something much more insidious and pervasive than racism that was also at play in the other cases we will examine and that is a **blind faith in the state** and therefore the cases it brings to trial. We discussed earlier how there has been a tectonic shift away from critical thinking and towards faith in the government's cases they bring against our fellow citizens and we deliver convictions 93% of the time we are presented with cases.

The comments themselves are racist, or at least racial, but what was driving it was that we were all barraged with pundits defending the state's case and telling us he was guilty. What I find interesting is that before the verdict even 40% of blacks thought he was guilty with 60% of African-Americans believing in his innocence. So the mainstream media even made headway indoctrinating the black population. However remember that the media made a point of only showing us blacks that thought OJ was innocent and almost every white pundit convinced of his guilt. So this is an example of how the media can actually get different messages to different segments of the population during the same programming.

To some degree we obviously do relate more to television personalities that share our race (and probably gender, hair color, etc. play a role to some degree). Remember that in every race only a small fraction of the population is committed to critical thinking or is even aware that there is a reason not to completely trust the news they are being given. I mean it does take some mental energy to see two races fighting on television and to say "you know the people that look like me and the people in my neighborhood are really wrong about this". There is a natural aversion to hold thoughts that will make you a pariah in your circles.

My family seemed to enjoy it though. One of the reasons we were so engrossed with the case was that my father had just recently sold his business when the OJ Simpson criminal trial got started and was effectively retired at a relatively young age. So he was able to watch every second of the trial at least once (because we would all watch the nightly rehashes and just marvel at how every detail would get twisted to fit into the state's case). So, I found it enjoyable to see my parents arguing with their friends about the cases. It was so obvious that most people didn't even really know why they thought OJ was guilty. It was really a matter of that the news had told them so.

It didn't matter that preservatives were found in nearly all of the blood that was found at OJ's residence. It didn't matter that **ten (10) witnesses** that paid close attention to OJ on his way to Chicago **saw NO GASH on his finger corroborating OJ's claim** that he got the small gash while in Chicago. Zero witnesses saw the gash until OJ was already on his way back from Chicago but the news thinks he's guilty so he must be guilty. The police don't go around arresting and framing innocent people (which may be true in most cases but that is where critical thinking breaks down since "most" cases have little to do with "this" case). Of course a few years later it comes out that the LAPD regularly would plant evidence to help cases along.

In the Rampart scandal more than **70 police officers** either assigned to or associated with the **Rampart CRASH unit** were implicated in some form of misconduct, making it one of the most widespread cases of documented police misconduct in United States history. The convicted offenses include unprovoked shootings, unprovoked beatings, **planting** of false evidence, **framing** of suspects, stealing and **dealing narcotics**, bank robbery, **perjury**, and the covering up of evidence of these activities.

Of course we did not have the benefit of this scandal being uncovered during the OJ Simpson trial but it should not have mattered. The OJ Simpson case was like the Rampart scandal in miniature. There was ETDA (a preservative used by crime scene units to preserve blood) present on the so-called "bloody" socks and in blood found at the crime scene; there was **more than enough blood missing** from a vile of OJ's blood (over 1.5 milliliters) to account for all of the blood found at his house and at Bundy; Nicole had blood under her fingers that could not have been OJ's, her own or Ron Goldman's (most likely belonging to the real killer); not to mention an astounding amount of evidence that the police admitted to taking with them from the crime scene to OJ's house – a practice that **breaks** from **LAPD procedures** and from common sense!

However, in this country you don't just throw out a case because you can prove that some of the evidence has been falsified. Across the pond it is another story. According to Giles Whittel of the UK based newspaper "The Times" the Simpson trial **should never have begun**. According to him "the sloppy police work at the crime scene, at Simpson's house and in his car contaminated the evidence so badly that **had it been a British case the Crown Prosecution Service** would have **rejected all of it**". Certainly if I were on the Jury the prosecution would have been in a major hole after trying to pass off planted evidence as real. And this is where race did play a role – not in the OJ case itself but in how the media was able to shape the public's reaction to it.

Listen, as an adult I have lived in some horrible neighborhoods in this country and in the third world where you can feel the tension between the police and the general public. I spent some time living in Harlem and even spent a year living in the projects while staying with a friend's family.

That said, I grew up in very nice mostly-white neighborhoods and I can see why it is difficult for people from those neighborhoods to imagine that a respected police officer planting evidence on someone.

**When you live in a nice neighborhood** you barely see the police (although when you call them they magically show up within minutes). When you do see them it is because they are getting in the middle of some domestic nonsense or it is when one of your neighbors just got robbed and they are there after the fact to fill out some paperwork. So as a result you just don't see police power being exerted against you or your neighbors. When they show up after you have been robbed **they are on your side**, they are just one of the good guys and you feel like they are keeping your neighborhood safe. The only time you hear people in rich neighborhoods complaining about police is when they get speeding tickets which they usually have no problem paying so all in all it is very easy to feel supportive of police and for good reason it is hard to imagine them as the bad guy.

Even in bad neighborhoods most police are out to just do their jobs but regardless of race the attitudes of the cops and the public are going to be different. Cops see some horrible things in bad neighborhoods and they start to get frustrated with their losing battle against crime and this is the point at which they may consider helping things along. Maybe it's something small like "I could see the contraband from the window before conducting the full search", or adding extra drugs to an actual drug bust to make sure they don't plead out to community service. Now both OJ and Nichol Brown-Simpson lived in marvelous neighborhoods but the cops handling the case were **LAPD** which cover some of the worst neighborhoods in the country.

So this begs the question: did Mark Fuhrman really see the tiny, almost microscopic, blood in the bronco before jumping over the fence into OJ's property? Is it unthinkable that he might have made that up and then added a drop or two later to make the story match? I don't think that is far-fetched at all. Also, it doesn't mean that OJ was framed in some grand conspiracy – it is much more likely that the police genuinely (but incorrectly) thought OJ was guilty and just helped the case along so to speak. Remember when a woman turns up dead it is usually the husband/ex-husband/boyfriend. Again, you and I both know that "usually" doesn't mean squat but I am trying to see things from all perspectives. Having a large amount of exposure to rich neighborhoods and ghettos I feel I am in a unique position to see this from all sides.

But again **I don't think OJ's race is what made him a target** of the LAPD. I say that because the Innocence Project regularly uncovers cases where absent or mishandled evidence has allowed defendants of all colors to end up wrongfully behind bars. He was the ex-husband, and they went with the "usual" rather than focus on the particulars of the case. Also, once the state gets the ball rolling in a certain direction it doesn't like to own up to the mistake and change direction. This manifests itself repeatedly within politics when the government spends millions trying to fix a problem only to make it worse and they say "well we tried to deal with substance abuse with setting up rehab centers and over 98% of the patients leaving them go right back to the substance abuse which is roughly the same result for users that don't go to rehab. That was a total failure so let's stop using tax payer money for this and try something else". No you will never see that. The state tries to take on a God-like quality and so they seem to want to cling to this mystique of infallibility.

## Blacker Than Black

That said the undercurrents of racial tensions were certainly played with by the media, the state and to some degree by the defense. Keep in mind much of the defense team's legitimate points got lumped into the race card by the media even though it was really the media that was pulling our strings when it came to our perceptions of race. One obvious example was when TIME Magazine ran a photo of OJ Simpson but augmented the photo to make OJ appear about ten shades darker than he was because the race baiters at TIME must have thought that would make him look guiltier. This may have gone unnoticed except for the fact that Newsweek decided to run the same photo without the doctoring (See Figure 1).

So with the OJ Simpson case we see the Jury acted logically and reasonably in coming to the verdict; when interviewed they didn't espouse any racist anti-white rhetoric nor did they expose any anti-police animus as the media would like you to believe. However, race was used repeatedly by the main stream media to fan the racial division in this country that would more likely than not fade into the background if the public was left to its own devices. But what about these other cases, namely that of Roderick Scott and George Zimmerman?

***Figure 1:** Time Magazine Plays With Race*

Now on the internet and even on television it seems that comparing the George Zimmerman case to any other trial automatically makes you a racist. Now for those of us that follow these legal dramas on a regular basis we know that all you can really do is compare the case to other cases. That is the whole basis of legal precedents – comparing the current case to the thousands of cases with a point of similarity. Now I have heard people referring to Roderick Scott as the "Black George Zimmerman" and I think that goes a little far and may be the reason for some of the backlash these comparisons are getting. The truth is that both sides are sort of right. The cases are very similar but they have their own unique points that we will get into in this volume.

The main difference though that is usually pointed out between the Scott and Zimmerman cases is that **they didn't arrest Zimmerman initially** (in fact one of the police officers testified that they didn't want to arrest him which I'm sure crushed the prosecutions already weak state) whereas Roderick Scott was arrested immediately after the police showed up. This is probably the biggest difference between the cases and is used to somehow show that it was racism that got Zimmerman off. If anything to me it would at most show racism against Roderick Scott and normal treatment for Zimmerman. But even that crumbles when you look closer at the details of the case. See, Zimmerman had been badly beaten up. He was bloodied up, with a broken nose and there was even a witness that Martin was on top of him beating him. To a police officer (or anyone versed in the law) this is really an open and shut case of self-defense. What information Zimmerman used to identify Martin as someone to stop and question in his community watch is completely irrelevant. If it was his dress, his manner, his race, his height, or his gender is completely irrelevant. Remember that besides being shot that Mr. Martin had no bruises, wounds or any other evidence of being beaten. That means that at the moment Zimmerman shot Martin in self-defense that Martin had been beating the crap out of Zimmerman and that Zimmerman had hardly touched him. This is why it is not hard to find black supporters of Zimmerman which I will get into later. My favorite quote was from Leo Terrell when he said "there was not a race case here at all… the jury got it right… **it's embarrassing for me as an African-American** to hear… MSNBC and CNN talk about this as a race case."

This was in an interchange between Juan Williams and Sean Hannity and astoundingly in the interchange Juan Williams (who is black if you are unfamiliar with the commentator) reveals that he disagreed with the OJ Simpson not guilty verdict. So Mr. Williams showed his implicit bias towards faith in the state and its prosecutors. **When Prosecutors Attack** they depend on this type of ingrained trust in the government. Mr. Williams, believes both in OJ Simpson's guilt and in George Zimmerman's guilt. And this is common today. I caught Levar Burton being interviewed and noticed that he was convinced of Zimmerman's guilt but also did not think OJ Simpson was innocent either. With regard to the OJ Simpson case it seems that the prevailing opinion among blacks that OJ Simpson was not guilty of murder has started to chip away

I was recently informed of a clip from the film "Barber Shop" where they have a segment where they talk about all the things "black people don't want to admit" and without providing any evidence to support this they make the statement that "OJ did it" and thus the power of entertainment. When you are being entertained you are much less critical of what you are being told. But he did seem to get it right about Rodney King and Jesse Jackson (if you've seen the movie then you know what I mean).

Getting back to the Roderick Scott case (unlike Zimmerman) he did not have a bruise on him which is why the police likely arrested him to sort out the details. Of course when you are defending yourself you do not need to wait until you have been injured to respond but that often gets sorted out after the arrest. The real shock in that case was that the prosecution went forward with no credible evidence to refute

Mr. Scott's claim of self-defense.

That said you always have grieving parents in these cases where a minor ends up dead. And I don't particularly blame the parents – I mean if my child ended up dead in an encounter with someone that is still alive I can't say I would be able to consider the facts objectively (which is why our justice system uses disinterested juries to decide these cases). Even so I can't imagine taking my child's side if his killer was badly beaten up and my child didn't have a bruise on him (but I guess you really can't tell until you are in that situation).

A minor dying from being shot, or from anything really, is such a tragedy that it easily garners the public's sympathy even if that tragedy was brought on by the minor's own actions. In the Zimmerman case you had one eye-witness that saw Martin on top of Zimmerman beating him; you had the bruises all over Zimmerman's body to corroborate the eye-witness testimony. There could hardly be more evidence to justify self-defense. I believe it is for these reasons that a chorus of blacks have come out in support of Zimmerman. We will get into this more later but here is just a short list of **blacks that have voiced their support** of George Zimmerman:

- Charles Barkley
- Larry Elder
- Joe Oliver
- Derryck Green
- Pastor Manning
- Leo Terrell
- Dr. Ben Carson
- Horace Cooper
- Armstrong Williams
- **Dr. Alveda King** (the niece of Dr. Martin Luther King, Jr. and she denounced the viral Photoshop-ed image depicting King in a hoodie).

In spite of what the mainstream media is trying to shove down your throat there are thousands of blacks that agree with the recent verdict giving Zimmerman back his freedom. I applaud the bravery of these individuals that are more committed to justice and thinking critically then to simply jumping on the racial bandwagon and calling for blood.

I was confounded by the President's comments that "Trayvon Martin could have been me 35 years ago". Really? I've read Obama's memoirs and while he openly admits to using all sorts of drugs and attending communist meetings I don't recall the chapter where he recounts beating up a Latino and breaking his nose! I don't recall him reminiscing about mounting a community watchman and slugging him MMA style either.

To Obama's credit he appears to have spent his youth trying to apply himself to his studies (when he wasn't experimenting with drugs). Not to mention that Obama was a **half-white community organizer** so it would have been more appropriate to say that **Zimmerman could have been him 25 years ago**.

I hope that it is starting to become clear that **When Prosecutors Attack** they don't seem to discriminate. This is really much scarier because it means that the problem is less isolated and less likely to abate even if we are becoming a "post-racial" country. Regardless of your race you could become a target of the police or an over eager prosecutor. It may not seem that way because the national media is only interested in cases that fit a template. The George Zimmerman case fit one of their favorite templates: White male gun-owner kills unarmed black guy.

## Tasers Don't Kill People, Cops with Tasers Kill People

By way of contrast you probably haven't heard about **the murder of Kelly Thomas**. The case of Kelly Thomas overlapped with the Trayvon Martin coverage and was a very simple case of a handful of police officers tasering a non-violent white vagrant to death. Not only that there was no question about what happened in this case because this abuse was caught on video tape. So where is the media coverage and subsequent national outrage? It doesn't exist because the government controlled media doesn't like these types of stories because it puts the focus on the out-of-control police state that is steadily coming into view.

Or how about **Danielle Maudsley** the 20-year old white suspect that was tasered running away from Florida law enforcement only to then fall down and crack her head on the pavement? She will likely be permanently brain damaged and is still in a coma. **Was she a threat to the police?** Well, let's see... she was unarmed, handcuffed and running away from police so make up your own mind on that one. Where were the "I am Danielle" marches? There was hardly any media attention so I am not surprised. Are these isolated cases? Hardly! Since 2001 roughly **541 people** have been <u>killed</u> by tasers in the United States alone.

Below are just a few names of which I guarantee you haven't heard.

These are **people of ALL races** that have been **killed by tasers**. Many of them were in custody or handcuffed. I didn't want to fill up the rest of the book so I've only included 190 cases but I could have included many more (see you on the other side):

Jan 9, 2009: Derrick Jones, 17, Black, Martinsville, Virginia
Jan 11, 2009: Rodolfo Lepe, 31, Hispanic, Bakersfield, California
Jan 22, 2009: Roger Redden, 52, Caucasian, Soddy Daisy, Tennessee-
Feb 2, 2009: Garrett Jones, 45, Caucasian, Stockton, California
Feb 11, 2009: Richard Lua, 28, Hispanic, San Jose, California
Feb 13, 2009: Rudolph Byrd, 37, Black, Thomasville, Georgia
Feb 13, 2009: Michael Jones, 43, Black, Iberia, Louisiana
Feb 14, 2009: Chenard Kierre Winfield, 32, Black, Los Angeles, California
Feb 28, 2009: Robert Lee Welch, 40, Caucasian, Conroe, Texas
Mar 22, 2009: Brett Elder, 15, Caucasian, Bay City, Michigan
Mar 26, 2009: Marcus D. Moore, 40, Black, Freeport, Illinois
Apr 1, 2009: John J. Meier Jr., 48, Caucasian, Tamarac, Florida
Apr 6, 2009: Ricardo Varela, 41, Hispanic, Fresno, California
Apr 10, 2009: Robert Mitchell, 16, Black, Detroit, Michigan
Apr 13, 2009: Craig Prescott, 38, Black, Modesto, California
Apr 16, 2009: Gary A. Decker, 50, Black, Tuscon, Arizona
Apr 18, 2009: Michael Jacobs Jr., 24, Black, Fort Worth, Texas
Apr 30, 2009: Kevin LaDay, 35, Black, Lumberton, Texas
May 4, 2009: Gilbert Tafoya, 53, Caucasian, Holbrook, Arizona
May 17, 2009: Jamaal Valentine, 27, Black, La Marque, Texas
May 23, 2009: Gregory Rold, 37, Black, Salem, Oregon
Jun 9, 2009: Brian Cardall, 32, Caucasian, Hurricane, Utah
Jun 13, 2009: Dwight Madison, 48, Black, Bel Air, Maryland
Jun 20, 2009 Derrek Kairney, 36, Race: Unknown, South Windsor, Connecticut
Jun 30, 2009, Shawn Iinuma, 37, Asian, Fontana, California
Jul 2, 2009, Rory McKenzie, 25, Black, Bakersfield, California
Jul 20, 2009, Charles Anthony Torrence, 35, Caucasian, Simi Valley, California
Jul 30, 2009, Johnathan Michael Nelson, 27, Caucasian, Riverside County, California
Aug 9, 2009, Terrace Clifton Smith, 52, Black, Moreno Valley, California
Aug 12, 2009, Ernest Ridlehuber, 53, Race: Unknown, Greenville, South Carolina
Aug 14, 2009, Hakim Jackson, 31, Black, Philadelphia, Pennsylvania
Aug 18, 2009, Ronald Eugene Cobbs, 38, Black, Greensboro, North Carolina
Aug 20, 2009, Francisco Sesate, 36, Hispanic, Mesa, Arizona
Aug 22, 2009, T.J. Nance, 37, Race: Unknown, Arizona City, Arizona
Aug 26, 2009, Miguel Molina, 27, Hispanic, Los Angeles, California
Aug 27, 2009, Manuel Dante Dent, 27, Hispanic, Modesto, California
Sep 3, 2009, Shane Ledbetter, 38, Caucasian, Aurora, Colorado
Sep 16, 2009, Alton Warren Ham, 45, Caucasian, Modesto, California
Sep 19, 2009, Yuceff W. Young II, 21, Black, Brooklyn, Ohio
Sep 21, 2009, Richard Battistata, 44, Hispanic, Laredo, Texas
Sep 28, 2009, Derrick Humbert, 38, Black, Bradenton, Florida

Oct 2, 2009, Rickey Massey, 38, Black, Panama City, Florida
Oct 12, 2009, Christopher John Belknap, 36, Race: Unknown, Ukiah, California
Oct 16, 2009, Frank Cleo Sutphin, 19, Caucasian, San Bernadino, California
Oct 27, 2009, Jeffrey Woodward, 33, Caucasian, Gallatin, Tennessee
Nov 13, 2009, Herman George Knabe, 58, Caucasian, Corpus Christi, Texas
Nov 14, 2009, Darryl Bain, 43, Black, Coram, New York
Nov 16, 2009, Matthew Bolick, 30, Caucasian, East Grand Rapids, Michigan
Nov 19, 2009, Jesus Gillard, 61, Black, Bloomfield Hills, Michigan
Nov 21, 2009, Ronald Petruney, 49, Race: Unknown, Washington, Pennsylvania
Nov 27, 2009, Eddie Buckner, 53, Caucasian, Chattanooga, Tennessee
Dec 11, 2009, Andrew Grande, 33, Caucasian, Oak County, Florida
Dec 11, 2009, Hatchel Pate Adams III, 36, Black, Hampton, Virginia
Dec 11, 2009, Paul Martin Martinez, 36, Hispanic, Roseville, California
Dec 13, 2009, Douglas Boucher, 39, Caucasian, Mason, Ohio
Dec 14, 2009, Linda Hicks, 62, Black, Toledo, Ohio
Dec 19, 2009, Preston Bussey III, 41, Black, Rockledge, Florida
Dec 20, 2009, Michael Hawkins, 39, Caucasian, Springfield, Missouri
Dec 30, 2009, Stephen Palmer, 47, Race: Unknown, Stamford, Connecticut
Jan 6, 2010, Delano Smith, 21, Black, Elkhart, Indiana
Jan 17, 2010, William Bumbrey III, 36, Black, Arlington, Virginia
Jan 20, 2010, Kelly Brinson, 45, Race: Unknown, Cincinnati, Ohio
Jan 27, 2010, Joe Spruill, Jr., Black, Goldsboro, North Carolina
Jan 28, 2010, Patrick Burns, 50, Caucasian, Sangamon County, Illinois
Jan 28, 2010, Daniel Mingo, 25, Black, Mobile, Alabama
Feb 4, 2010, Mark Morse, 36, Caucasian, Phoenix, Arizona
Mar 4, 2010, Roberto Olivo, 33, Hispanic, Tulare, California
Mar 5, 2010, Christopher Wright, 48, Race: Unknown, Seattle, Washington
Mar 10, 2010, Jaesun Ingles, 31, Black, Midlothian, Illinois
Mar 10, 2010, James Healy Jr., 44, Race: Unknown, Rhinebeck, New York
Mar 20, 2010, Albert Valencia, 31, Hispanic, Downey, California
Apr 10, 2010, Daniel Joseph Barga, 24, Caucasian, Cornelius, Oregon
Apr 30, 2010, Adil Jouamai, 32, Moroccan, Arlington, Virginia
May 9, 2010, Audreacus Davis, 29, Black, Atlanta, Georgia
May 14, 2010, Sukeba Olawunmi, 39, Race: Unknown, Atlanta, Georgia
May 24, 2010, Efrain Carrion, 35, Hispanic, Middletown, Connecticut
May 27, 2010, Carl Johnson, 48, Caucasian, Baltimore, Maryland
May 29, 2010, Jose Martinez, 53, Hispanic, Waukegan, Illinois
May 31, 2010, Anastasio Hernández Rojas, 42, Hispanic, San Ysidro, California
Jun 8, 2010, Terrelle Houston, 22, Black, Hempstead, Texas
Jun 12, 2010, Curtis Robinson, 34, Black, Albuquerque, New Mexico
Jun 13, 2010, William Owens, 17, Race: Unknown, Homewood, Alabama
Jun 14, 2010, Jose Alfredo Jimenez, 42, Hispanic, Harris County, Texas
Jun 15, 2010, Michael White, 47, Black, Vallejo, California
Jun 22, 2010, Daniel Sylvester, 35, Caucasian, Crescent City, California
July 5, 2010, Damon Falls, 31, Black, Oklahoma City, Oklahoma
July 5, 2010, Edmund Gutierrez, 22, Hispanic, Imperial, California
July 8, 2010, Phyllis Owens, 87, Race: Unknown, Clackamas County, Oregon

July 9, 2010, Marvin Booker, 56, Race: Black, Denver, Colorado
July 12, 2010, Anibal Rosario-Rodriguez, 61, Hispanic, New Britain, Connecticut
July 15, 2010, Jerome Gill, Race: Unknown, Chicago, Illinois
July 18, 2010, Edward Stephenson, 46, Race: Unknown, Leavenworth, Kansas
July 23, 2010, Jermaine Williams, 30, Black, Cleveland, Mississippi
Aug 1, 2010, Dennis Sandras, 49, Race: Unknown, Houma, Louisiana
Aug 9, 2010, Andrew Torres, 39, Hispanic, Greenville, South Carolina
Aug 18, 2010, Martin Harrison, 50, Caucasian, Dublin, California
Aug 19, 2010, Adam Disalvo, 30, Caucasian, Daytona Beach, Florida
Aug 20, 2010, Stanley Jackson, 31, Black, Washtenaw County, Michigan
Aug 24, 2010, Michael Ford, 50, Black, Livonia, Michigan
Aug 25, 2010, Eduardo Hernandez-Lopez, 21, Hispanic, Las Vegas, Nevada
Aug 31, 2010, King Hoover, 27, Black, Spanaway, Washington
Sep 4, 2010, Adam Colliers, 25, Caucasian, Gold Bar, Washington
Sep 10, 2010, Larry Rubio, 20, Race: Unknown, Leemore, California
Sep 12, 2010, Freddie Lockett, 30, Black, Dallas, Texas
Sep 16, 2010, Gary L. Grossenbacher, 48, Race: TBA, Oklahoma City, Oklahoma
Sep 18, 2010, David Cornelius Smith, 28, Black, Minneapolis, Minnesota
Sep 18, 2010, Joseph Frank Kennedy, 48, Caucasian, La Mirada, California
Oct 4, 2010, Javon Rakestrau, 28, Black, Lafayette Parish, Louisiana
Oct 7, 2010, Patrick Johnson, 18, Caucasian, Philadelphia, Pennsylvania
Oct 12, 2010, Ryan Bain, 31, Caucasian, Billings, Montana
Oct 14, 2010, Karreem Ali, 65, Black, Silver Spring, Maryland
Oct 19, 2010, Troy Hooftallen, 36, Caucasian, Punxsutawney, Pennsylvania
Nov 4, 2010, Eugene Lamott Allen, 40, Race: Unknown, Wilmington, Delaware
Nov 6, 2010, Robert Neill, Jr., 61, Caucasian, Mount Joy, Pennsylvania
Nov 7, 2010, Mark Shaver, 32, Caucasian, Brimfield, Ohio
Nov 23, 2010, Denevious Thomas, 36, Black, Albany, Georgia
Nov 26, 2010, Rodney Green, 36, Black, Waco, Texas
Nov 27, 2010, Blaine McElroy, 37, Race: Unknown, Jackson County, Mississippi
Dec 2, 2010, Clayton Early James, Race: Unknown, Elizabeth City, North Carolina
Dec 11, 2010, Anthony Jones, 44, Race: Unknown, Las Vegas, Nevada
Dec 12, 2010, Linel Lormeus, 26, Black, Naples, Florida
Dec 20, 2010, Christopher Knight, 35, Black, Brunswick, Georgia
Dec 31, 2010, Rodney Brown, 40, Black, Cleveland, Ohio
Jan 5, 2011, Kelly Sinclair, 41, Race: Unknown, Amarillo, Texas
Feb 5, 2011, Robert Ricks, 23, Black, Alexandria, Louisiana
March 15, 2011, Brandon Bethea, 24, Black, Harnett County, North Carolina
Apr 3, 2011, Jairious McGhee, 23, Black, Tampa, Florida
Apr 22, 2011, Adam Spencer Johnson, 33, Caucasian, Orlando, Florida
Apr 23, 2011, Ronald Armstrong, 43, Race: Unknown, Pinehurst, North Carolina
Apr 25, 2011, Kevin Darius Campbell, 39, Race: Unknown, Tallahassee, Florida
May 1, 2011, Marcus Brown, 26, Black, Waterbury, Connecticut
May 6, 2011, Matthew Mittelstadt, 56, Caucasian, Boundary County, Idaho
May 11, 2011, Allen Kephart, 43, Caucasian, San Bernadino County, California
June 13, 2011, Howard Hammon, 41, Caucasian, Middleburg, Ohio
June 22, 2011, Otto Kolberg, 55, Caucasian, Waycross, Georgia

June 28, 2011, Dalric East, 40, Black, Montgomery County, Maryland
July 5, 2011, Kelly Thomas, 37, Caucasian, Fullerton, California
July 10, 2011, Joshua Nossoughi, 32, Caucasian, Springfield, Missouri
July 19, 2011, Alonzo Ashley, 29, Black, Denver, Colorado
July 21, 2011, La'Reko Williams, 21, Black, Charlotte, North Carolina
July 30, 2011, Donald Murray, 39, Caucasian, Westland, Michigan
August 4, 2011, Pierre Abernathy, 30, Black, San Antonio, Texas
August 6, 2011, Everette Howard, 18, Black, Cincinnati, Ohio
August 6, 2011, Debro Wilkerson, 29, Black, Prince William County, Maryland
August 6, 2011, Gregory Kralovetz, 50, Caucasian, Kaukauna, Wisconsin
August 12, 2011, Joseph Lopez, 49, Hispanic, Santa Barbara, California
August 17, 2011, Roger Chandler, 41, Caucasian, Helena, Montana
August 21, 2011, Montalito McKissick, 37, Black, Oklahoma City, Oklahoma
August 24, 2011, Michael Evans, 56, Race: Unknown, Fayetteville, North Carolina
August 30, 2011, Nicholas Koscielniak, 27, Caucasian, Lancaster, New York
September 11, 2011, Tyree Sinclair, 31, Black, Corpus Christi, Texas
September 13, 2011, Damon Barnett, 44, Caucasian, Fresno, California
September 17, 2011, Richard Kokenos, 27, Caucasian, Warren, Michigan
September 24, 2011, Bradford Gibson, 35, Black, Mt. Pleasant, Michigan
September 24, 2011, Donacio Rendon, 43, Race: Unknown, Lubbock, Texas
September 29, 2011, Howard Cook, 35, Black, York, Pennsylvania
October 4, 2011, Glenn Norman, 46, Caucasian, Camden County, Missouri
October 9, 2011, Darnell Hutchinson, 32, Black, San Leandro, California
October 31, 2011, Chad Brothers, 32, Caucasian, Colonie, New York
November 6, 2011, Darrin Hanna, 43, Black, North Chicago, Illinois
November 13, 2011, Ronald Cristiano, 51, Caucasian, Bridgeport, Connecticut
November 15, 2011, Jonathan White, 29, Black, San Bernardino, California
November 22, 2011, Roger Anthony, 61, Black, Scotland Neck, North Carolina
December 16, 2011, Marty Atencio, 44, Hispanic, Phoenix, Arizona
December 22, 2011, Wayne Williams, 27, Black, Houma, Louisiana
January 15, 2012, Daniel Guerra, 24, Hispanic, Ft. Worth, Texas
February 29, 2012, Raymond Allen, 34, Black, Galveston, Texas
March 5, 2012, Nehemiah Dillard, 29, Black, Gainesville, Florida
March 12, 2012, Jersey Green, 37, Black, Aurora, Illinois
March 19, 2012, James Barnes, 38, Caucasian, Pinellas County, Florida
April 10, 2012, Bobby Merrill, 38, Black, Saginaw, Michigan
April 21, 2012, Angel Heraldo, 41, Hispanic, Meriden, Connecticut
April 22, 2012, Bruce Chrestensen, 52, Caucasian, Grass Valley, California
May 10, 2012, Damon Abraham, 34, Black, Baldwin, Louisiana
June 9, 2012, Randolph Bonvillian, 41, Caucasian, Houma, Louisiana
June 20, 2012, Macadam Mason, 39, Caucasian, Thetford, Vermont
June 30, 2012, Victor Duffy, 25, Black, Tukwila, Washington
July 1, 2012, Corey McGinnis, 35, Black, Cincinnati, Ohio
July 5, 2012, Sampson Castellane, 29, Native American, Fife, Washington
September 1, 2012, Denis Chabot, 38, Caucasian, Houston, Texas
September 14, 2012, Bill Williams, 60, Caucasian, Everett, Washington
November 29, 2012, Robert Maurina, 46, Caucasian, West Allis, Wisconsin

December 13, 2012, Philip Coleman, 38, Black, Chicago, Illinois
December 25, 2012, Kevin Culp, 29, Black, Richmond, Washington
January 1, 2013, Andrew Layton, 26, Caucasian, Mankato, Minnesota
February 23, 2013, Christopher Parker, 33, Caucasian, Spokane, Washington
April 19, 2013, Anthony Howard, 51, Black, Gaithersburg, Maryland
July 21, 2013, Deomain Hayman, 28, Black, Wilmington, Delaware
July 24, 2013, Daimon Simmons, 29, Unknown, Middle Island, New York
July 26, 2013, John Varna, 95, Unknown, Forest Park, Illinois

**I'm sure you are blown away by this list** as I was when I uncovered this in my research. Did you notice that I'm not pulling junk out from the 1970's when Tasers first came into circulation here? Instead I've chosen to mention **just the cases I could find since 2009** (which I hope helps the rah-rah "police are great" crowd take a moment to reflect on this since these all occurred under Obama – it's a funny thing when you try and reach everyone you risk alienating *everyone* and reaching *no one* but again I respect the intelligence of anyone that would search out a book of this nature).

Notice that every time a case of police brutality becomes national news that there is always a racial component because this perfectly polarizes the nation. Al Sharpton and Jesse Jackson quickly claim the event was racially motivated and this resonates with people that live in neighborhoods with high amounts of police action. On the other side of the spectrum whites tend to identify with the police – imagining themselves, their husbands or sons being on the beat and having to negotiate a situation with a possibly homicidal criminal. But if the **Kelly Thomas** story became national news there would be no polarization. Instead the public would have a united sentiment against this type of police action. There would be no other angle that could be taken (unless someone has the gall to advocate tasering vagrants to death). Perhaps we would start to **question the use of non-lethal weaponry** which (although being less lethal) **lowers the bar** that allows police to attack citizens at large and can indeed be lethal as was the case with Kelly Thomas. I mean the bar has been lowered to such a degree that even non-violent grandmothers, old ladies, and 8-months pregnant women are being tasered and no one seems to care!

But that sort of questioning would upset this seemingly relentless move to becoming a police state with militarized police forces donning futuristic looking riot gear. Instead we are shown movie after movie and TV show after TV show that make light of being tased. Thousands of volts running through someone's nervous system is absolutely not funny. That hasn't stopped the propaganda from flowing and getting unsuspecting audiences repeatedly laughing at someone being tased and at times being forced to relieve themselves in public. It is truly disgusting if you think about it.

So I think at this point we haven't got the elephant out of the room but we have at least addressed it. I think by now you should get the sense that I acknowledge that race is a divisive issue today but that putting everything into racial terms is very foreign to me personally. Also, I sympathize with members of all races **When Prosecutors Attack** them when there is no evidence. It should also be clear that I have no gripe with law enforcement in general but that I am not blind to the abuses (although I have trouble viewing it in racial terms when I see lists like the above).

If you are white and convinced of OJ Simpson's guilt or if you are black and convinced of Zimmerman's culpability, I hope that you will still be able to hear me out and objectively review the evidence provided in all three cases. Remember, regardless of your race you could be the upcoming target **When Prosecutors Attack** next!

# UNIT ONE: OJ SIMPSON

# **OJ SIMPSON:** NOT LIKE THE OTHERS

## Which One of These Cases is Not Like the Other?

If you were exposed to Sesame Street growing up then you are likely familiar with the jingle "which one of these things is not like the other". Obviously, the George Zimmerman case is the hot case that is still fresh on everyone's mind. Since it is on everyone's mind comparisons start to be made to previous cases (and as we discussed earlier this isn't some white man's plot specific to this cases but is always done on high profile cases). Obviously no case is going to be identical to this case. The closest analog I could find was that of the Roderick Scott case that we will be getting into later.

I've chosen to profile the OJ Simpson case in this volume for many reasons. Partly because there are several important similarities; partly because there are some important distinctions; and also partly because in four years it looks like **OJ Simpson** will be set free and I am hoping to reach as many people as possible before then so that **maybe (just maybe) this innocent man can have some peace** when he gets out.

## Things Uncommon

The particulars of the OJ Simpson trial really could not be more different than the George Zimmerman case (and therefor from the Roderick Scott case).

First, in the OJ case there was no question that the deceased in question were in fact murdered (and not just killed in self-defense as was the case in the Scott and Zimmerman cases). Also, those killed at Bundy were adults whereas the Scott and Zimmerman cases held the added weight of having minors involved.

So since two murders definitely took place (*no one is claiming Goldman and Nichole Brown were killed in self-defense, or committed suicide, etc.*) the forensic evidence became central to the case. So, had I not included this case we would be missing a major tactic that is typical **When Prosecutors Attack** and that is messing with forensic evidence. Prosecutors seem brazenly willing to withhold vital information, present tainted evidence, twist lab results and the worst part is that, more times than not, defendants simply do not have the resources they would need to refute all of their specious prosecutorial attacks.

Another major difference is that OJ Simpson **was already famous** before the incident. Unlike Zimmerman and Scott, that you never heard of prior to the unfortunate incidents that they are now associated with, OJ Simpson had not only fame but the funds needed to counter all of the prosecution's dirty tricks that we will get into later. No matter how much money you have you can't really nullify evidence unless you can get through a Judge or make a convincing case to a Jury. So having money does not get a guilty man off (unfortunately conversely not having money **can** cause an innocent man to get convicted if his swamped public defender doesn't catch fabricated evidence). That being said a rich man has never been executed in the United States but that is a separate matter altogether.

Another difference between the cases is that Roderick Scott and George Zimmerman faced all-white and mostly-white juries respectively However, I really do believe that more is made of this than is warranted. Especially in the OJ Simpson case the jurors were sequestered even from watching the news. I remember thinking that this was harsh but after investigating these three cases I can see how powerful and twisted the media can be. I believe that **had the jury been all-white** (instead of just a quarter white) **AND sequestered** that they would have come to the same verdict of Not Guilty. I say this because the vast majority of whites that watched the actual trial (and didn't get their information from Nancy dis-Grace and the other airhead pundits) ended up agreeing with the verdict. However, if they were allowed to view the poisonous propaganda each night that programmed whites to think one thing and blacks to think another (to polarize a country that was previously roaring towards peacefully integrated race relations) then that would be another matter.

How the police conducted themselves in the OJ Simpson case is the last major difference that is worth mentioning. In the Roderick Scott and Zimmerman cases the **police seem to have acted honorably** and according to procedure. They didn't plant evidence, contaminate the crime scene, violate the fourth amendment by conducting unwarranted searches, commit perjury in open court, and they didn't throw standard police and forensic procedures out the window. In other words, they seem to have acted honorably and both the Zimmerman and Scott cases were pure cases of **When Prosecutors Attack**, but in the OJ Simpson case it seems that the LAPD was also on the attack for whatever reason.

I think it is worthwhile to take a moment and talk about the LAPD's motives for breaking standard police procedures, tearing up the constitution and at least partially fabricating evidence. I don't think that you can claim that this is all racially motivated. Yes, Mark Fuhrman was an actual racist. There is just no way around that one. I really do despise how much claims of racism are made in the media and on the internet. I'm sure I will get accused of it at some point by some mindless drone. Using the N-word is not at all proof that someone is racist and to be honest nor is someone making an off color or tasteless joke (that's just proof of being tasteless). But when you start talking about a certain race having a horrible stench or admitting to beating N's that you have in custody because the bruises don't show up because of their skin color… then it starts to become impossible to claim that you don't have problems with race.

More damning then all that is **Mark Fuhrman's own disability claim** in which he tells psychiatrists that **he had tortured suspects and "hated niggers"**. Fuhrman was seeking stress disability commonly referred to as "psycho pensions". What I find oddly comical is that the defense team had an internal memorandum where they state that the prosecution **wouldn't dare call this officer** to the stand. The astonishing thing is that the onus somehow got switched onto the defense team – that somehow they were the ones "playing the race card" that we all have heard repeated ad nausea. It wasn't the defense team's fault that he admitted to torturing suspects into offering confessions, hating blacks and beating them up while in custody.

See it wasn't just that he was using the N-word like the media made it into; rather it was HOW the N-word was being used. To illustrate this I am going to show you several damning passages from Fuhrman's comments – only I am going to substitute the "N-word" for the nonderogatory term of "black" (and if you think "black" is offensive you've probably already stopped reading my book anyhow) so you can see what I mean:

- In explaining the demographic makeup of the LAPD Fuhrman said "That we've got females ...and **dumb [blacks]**, and all your Mexicans that can't even write the name of the car they drive."
- In explaining an arrest Fuhrman made in Westwood: "**He was a [black]. He didn't belong**. Two questions. And you are going: Where do you live? 22nd and Western. Where were you going? Well, I'm going to Fatburger. Where's Fatburger. He didn't know where Fatburger was? Get in the [police] car."
- This is what Fuhrman had to say about American aid to drought victims in Ethiopia: "You know these people here; we got all this money going to Ethiopia for what? **To feed a bunch of dumb [blacks]** that their own government won't even feed."
- Discussing working in the Valley: "It's pretty clear-cut who the a**holes are. You go to Pacoima; you got bikers and [blacks]."

Now I am really not overly sensitive when it comes to racial comments. When I hear someone say something about Puerto Ricans or Jews (which are part of my ethnic makeup) I try and distinguish between a "racial" and "racist" comment if you know what I mean. For something to be racist it really has to have a component of hate in it that is not always there when people cry racism. But in the above comments – even with me removing the all-powerful N-word – you still cannot escape the **racially twisted perspective** of this so-called officer.

This is the officer that miraculously found both gloves during the "investigation", one at Bundy and one on OJ's property. What's more he did not wait to get a search warrant and instead made the ridiculous claim that he was concerned for OJ's safety at the time and that this substantiated his claim of there being exigent circumstances. Right. You know the fourth amendment is there for a reason. Had he waited for a warrant enough time would likely have passed so that more officers would have been around so that he could not plant the second glove (that's if the judge would have granted such a warrant which I highly doubt).

But people will say "what possible reason could Mark Fuhrman have for taking such a risky step". This hackneyed quip is so ridiculous that it is hard to know even where to start. First, of all – putting racism aside – Fuhrman had everything to gain by becoming a central figure in this case evidenced by the fact that he has made **millions** publishing several books where he can capitalize on his infamy. Secondly, he has been quoted (by Kathleen Bell) as saying that **if he saw an interracial couple** driving he would pull them over and find a reason to take one of them in. Also according to her he stated that if he had it his way "they would take all the [blacks], put them together in a big group and burn them". Again I took out the N-word so you can judge what he is actually saying without that inflammatory slur but it seems that besides personal gain race might – just might – have played a factor here.

It is not without a touch of irony that Fuhrman **performed a warrantless search** (effectively nullifying Mr. Simpson's fourth amendment protection against unreasonable searches), that he **admits to beating out confessions** (thus canceling the suspects fifth amendment right not to incriminate himself) and to top it all off Mr. Fuhrman then relies on the fifth amendment himself when asked **"have you ever falsified a police report"** and "did you plant or manufacture any evidence in ***this*** case" (not to mention that people STILL refer to the glove as if this is a valid piece of evidence).

The fact that the gloves didn't fit with thin latex gloves on was irrelevant in light of the above. Interestingly, F. Lee Baily points out that the Jury came out after the verdict and said that the gloves not fitting did NOT hit home with them. They (like the media) factored in that the gloves might have fit without the interior latex gloves. Now I am originally from the Northeast and have owned more than one pair of fine leather gloves. I never owned a pair of gloves that would not have fit had I been wearing latex gloves. That's just not how people buy those gloves – usually people account for the fact that you might have an extra cloth glove inside for when it is really cold so you leave some room there.

Also, there have been claims that the gloves shrunk which is ridiculous because any fine pair of gloves that OJ would buy would be pre-shrunk. Understandably, most people might miss this detail but if you have been around well-to-do men that like fine clothing, steak houses and aged scotch like OJ (and the men in the community I grew up in) did then you just take this for granted. He was always impeccably dressed and likely never stepped foot in a Burlington Coat factory in his whole adult life.

I think Alan Dershowitz (who has otherwise been a horrible post-verdict advocate for Simpson) summed up Mark Fuhrman rather nicely:

> "They put on a policeman who **was a Nazi lover and a perjurer and an evidence planter**. That made our day, as the defense."

So I hope you can see the value of discussing the OJ Simpson case even based on the differences (not in spite of them). I want to first establish with the OJ case that I do accept that at times the police (or rather certain police officers) can be corrupt and even act out of racially motivated perspectives; I am hoping this will give me some credibility with the reader that is approaching this subject as a Trayvon Martin supporter. We have to have some common ground and the most appalling case of police misconduct in recent memory was certainly the OJ Simpson trial. Had people taken the defense more seriously in that case then the Rampart scandal could have come out during the trial and not years later. The **real injustice** there is that when the Rampart scandal hit the news all the pundits that had compared the idea of cops framing OJ as bad science fiction weren't made to eat crow.

Also, as we discussed above you can see that I don't claim any direct parallels between these cases (every case is different) so with that in mind I think we can approach the similarities with more of an open mind then what I have been seeing in the liberal blogosphere.

## Common Ground

Now that we have acknowledged the apparent differences lets discuss where these cases have points of similarity. When examining these areas keep in mind that it is not just these three cases that share this unfortunate common ground but that this is simply par for the course **When Prosecutors Attack** and attack they do

**When Prosecutors Attack** a private citizen the mainstream media gets on board with the State's message. This was certainly the case in the OJ Simpson and George Zimmerman cases.

In the OJ Simpson case the media would repeat the States assertion that there was a "mountain of evidence" which was really more of a molehill made up of blood containing a preservative added by crime scene investigators, some hairs that could easily have come from the blanket the bone head cops covered Nicole at the crime scene with and gloves that were too small and "discovered" by the same cop that found the glove at Bundy and pleaded the fifth when asked if he planted evidence in this case!

In the George Zimmerman case everything you heard from the mainstream media was wrong from the outset. They claimed that he was on his community watch shift (to fit into their wannabe cop template) when in fact he saw Martin on his way back from Target. But the prosecution/media duo is very careful about what information it releases and they know that most people shop at Target but almost no one participates in a community watch program (we are all too lazy for that – myself included). See most of the impressions we get from the media have less to do with evidence and facts and much more to do with identifying with the players in a story at an emotional level.

**When Prosecutors Attack** you will also notice that the prosecutors will play with photos. They will release bogus photos, withhold any photos that implicate other suspects or put the defendant in a favorable light and release photos that endear the public to the victim or alleged victim.

## Media Abuse

How did this manifest itself in the Simpson case? Well, for one everyone has an impression that OJ Simpson was an abusive husband. Of course abuse doesn't equate to murder but that is beside the point. The fact is that OJ Simpson **was not abusive** or rather he **did not "hit" Nicole**. This may seem shocking to you but remember how the prosecution contaminated the public opinion with fabricated photos? No? Well, take a look at the following that the prosecution released to the media (but of course did not submit as evidence) to paint OJ Simpson as an abusive husband even though they knew **this photo was taken on a movie set** and that **the bruises are all makeup!**

***Figure 2:*** *Swelling and Bruises Done By Makeup Artist on Movie Set*

## Postcards from an Alternate Reality

In fact, while there may have been several calls to the police there was only one documented "incident" where any actual harm to Nicole Brown Simpson was officially recorded. Now I know how touchy and explosive this type of issue is so let me just say that I am married and the idea of hitting a woman to harm her makes my stomach turn. This issue is so touchy that the defense simply said that abuse does not prove murder and gingerly pointed out that most of the abuse case the prosecution was building lacked foundation. They had eight women on the jury so the defense team proceeded as if they were walking through a mine field. I mean if by trying to prove he was not abusive (which he was not being charged for) they left the Jury with the impression that he was a callously unrepentant abuser that would have been a big loser. They went with the bird in hand rather than chasing two in the bush and just moved on.

That said there is a difference between getting scuffed up and being beaten and it is simply an insult to truly battered women to put Nicole in that same category. OJ, even past his physical prime, was a paragon of physical power. Had he really beat her she would have sustained severe injuries that were simply never documented. Here are the actual real photos taken from the only documented "abuse" case from 1989 (the most disturbing part of the picture is her facial expression):

***Figure 3:*** *These Pictures are Real But What is Shown?*

So the first photo we showed remember was a completely fraudulent photo that came from a movie set (where a professional makeup artist was practicing on Nicole while OJ was shooting a movie). The pictures in **Figure** are real but what do they show? Certainly they do not show a woman that has been "beaten" by one of the most powerful football players in history. Someone beaten by OJ – especially a small framed model type like Nicole – would be unrecognizable. I know that no one – even OJ advocates – want to touch this subject but that is exactly why I must. The children they had together should have at least one voice that is giving their father and her ex-husband a fair shake.

Remember this is a man that Nicole welcomed into her home to play games of monopoly with the kids and for family functions as recently as a few weeks before her passing. Forget a few weeks, I mean the same day of the killings his demeanor and relationship to the Brown family was captured by an amateur videographer (really just someone with a camera that was there to video *their* kids recital) and the New York Times describes it as follows:

> *"Mr. Simpson is seen laughing as he good-naturedly picked up his son, and then* ***was kissed by Ms. Brown and her mother****, Juditha. Mr. Simpson is also seen shaking hands with his former wife's father, Louis Brown, and joking with a friend."*

Now I am a father, in fact I have daughter and there is just no way that I'm going to have that type of relationship with a man that brutalized my precious daughter. Now if they had a minor scuffle and my daughter called police and used it to extract a very comfortable divorce settlement then I'd have no problem shaking the man's hand. The truth is that the photos in **Figure** are the result of a 1989 New Year's incident in which they were fighting about who knows what… he kicked her out of the house and she was trying to get back inside to continue their petty spat and OJ grabs her firmly by the arms and tosses her out of the house at which point she stumbles down a few porch steps and falls down getting mud on her pants and some very mild bruising as you see depicted in **Figure** .

From this point on Nicole milked this as far as she could. Based on this she calls police, hides behind a bush (instead of fleeing the premises as you would do if you were in fear of your life) and pops out and tells cops "He is trying to kill me" or something to that affect and gets that on a police report. Later she gets O.J. to agree that if he ever hits her it will cancel their prenuptial agreement (thus awarding her half of his then sizable fortune). It is for this reason that she started making those journal entries, why she saved the misleading photo found in **Figure 2**, and it explains the 911 calls. I know that every author that has come before me has danced around this issue because they don't want to "speak ill of the dead" or for some other reason don't come right out and lay it on the line but she was out for the money.

In fact, OJ's agreement to effectively tear up the prenuptial agreement if he ever hit her in the future is really proof to me that from 1989 until Nicole's untimely demise OJ didn't lay a hand on her. How can I say that? Well, if he had she would have had everything to gain by reporting it and collecting her millions (15 million actually). Steven H. Adler in his book entitled "Justice Defeated: Victims: OJ Simpson and the American Legal System" put it this way:

> "*…the strong reasons that I believe O.J.* **did not** *commit the murders, the*

> ***prenuptial agreement.*** *In the letters he agrees to amend the prenuptial agreement to stipulate he would forfeit half of his net worth if he ever hit her again. It is this agreement that gives suspicion to Nicole's [journal] claims of being hit. If she were to be hit again, all her frantic money problems would be solved." (bolding ours)*

Now the only problem I have with the above quote is the term "hit again" suggesting that OJ hit her in the first place. His agreement was actually worded to say if he ever hit her in the future then she would be entitled to half. Future is different than "again" because future doesn't concede it ever occurred. Sounds like a game with words but the point is that OJ took responsibility for the bruises in Figure 3 and eventually accepted that it fell under the category of "battery" but that is not the same thing as him hitting her. I'm reminded of the case when Mike Tyson delivered a single blow to the street fighter Mitch Green. Do you remember how badly Green looked after just being hit once (and he was much more evenly matched)? If you have forgotten here is a picture of this single blow:

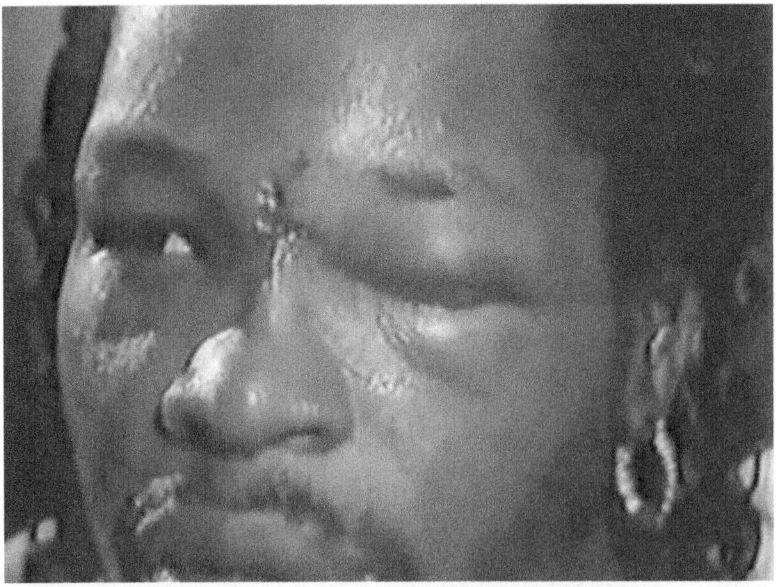

***Figure 4:*** *When a Powerful Athlete Punches You*

I do understand that Figure 4 is not directly related to the facts of this case but before you go trolling the blogosphere looking to hate on me try and hear what I am saying. When you compare this to Figure 3 it becomes obvious that Mitch Green was hit and that Nicole Brown was not hit in the face by OJ, it just never happened. Not on New Year's Day 1989 and most certainly not after he amended the prenuptial agreement or she would have collected her millions. The only photo that shows Nicole looking anything like Mitch Green in Figure 4 is the manufactured photo in Figure 2 that again came from a movie set makeup artist. Johnny Cochran said it in his closing statements: "since 1989 to now there was never any physical violence between OJ Simpson and Nicole Brown Simpson".

Of course, since OJ had declared No Contest to the 1989 abuse charge Johnny Cochran decided not to try and pick the isolated incident apart as I have here. It's not nice to toss someone out of your house causing them to get a little bruise but he did not hit her and (unless you grew up on non-stop made for Lifetime movies) it is a reach to say that OJ "abused" his wife (just so you know it was my wife – who has had to comfort victims of **real domestic abuse** – that pressed this point that I would have otherwise omitted from this volume). The following excerpt from a police interrogation conducted by Philip Vannatter and Thomas Lange really says it all:

> VANNATTER: How long were you together?
> **SIMPSON**: Seventeen years.
> VANNATTER: Seventeen years. Did you ever hit her, O.J.?
> **SIMPSON**: Ah, one night we had a fight. We had a fight and she hit me. And they never took my statement, they never wanted to hear my side, and **they never wanted to hear the housekeeper's side**. Nicole was drunk. She did her thing, she started tearing up my house, you know? I didn't punch her or anything, but I...
> VANNATTER: [You] slapped her a couple of times.
> **SIMPSON**: No, no, I wrestled her, is what I did. I didn't slap her at all. I mean, Nicole's a strong girl. She's a... one of the most conditioned women. Since that period of time, she's hit me a few times, but I've never **touched** her after that, and I'm telling you, its five-six years ago.

So, OJ maintains that he never hit (or even slapped) Nicole but what I find much more compelling is the fact that they never took his statement and that the housekeeper was present but never questioned by police. Remember this is the same housekeeper that testified in the criminal trial that on the night of the Bundy murders OJ's infamous Bronco was parked in front of Rockingham all night.

See this is just one example of how **When Prosecutors Attack** an unreality is created in the minds of the general public and manipulating the use of photos is crucial to this deception. The very same thing occurred in the prosecution of George Zimmerman. How so?

First, they decided to circulate a photo of Trayvon Martin from several years before the incident when he looked much younger[1]. Normally this would not be such a big deal except the media was running with the idea that Zimmerman had shot a "child" and obscured the fact that Martin was significantly taller than Zimmerman.

Secondly, and more importantly the prosecution dragged their heals before releasing the all-important color photo of Zimmerman with a bloodied up (and possibly broken) nose. The unfortunate shooting took place on February 26th 2012 however this vital photo was not released until December **over nine months** later! Our internal pages are greyscale so including that photo here would be meaningless (but a thumbnail color version is part of our cover design) but I am sure by now you are already familiar with it anyhow. This photo is evidence that Martin had committed a crime and that he had battered Zimmerman providing more than enough justification for him to defend himself. Combine this with the fact that Martin had no bruises or any other signs of being beaten by George Zimmerman prior to the shooting death.

In other words, this wasn't so much a fight as much as George Zimmerman getting pulverized until he could reach for his gun. Some people have said that George should have tried to get an arm free to hit Martin instead of mortally wound him. Of course these people were not there having their heads beaten into concrete but it is worth mentioning that if Zimmerman had bruised up Martin as he was being bruised up it would be impossible after the fact to forensically determine who was picking a fight on who. What I mean is that since we know that all of the bruises Zimmerman suffered were prior to him shooting Martin (since the gun shot was fatal) then we know that – at least physically – the attack was initiated by Martin.

The manipulation of photos doesn't end there but we will pick that up in the section on Zimmerman. The point is that we all know that a picture tells a thousand words but the unfortunate truth is that **When Prosecutors Attack** pictures can tell a thousand lies (although often just one or two strategic lies will suffice with the media filling in the gaps for them).

---

[1] Martin died a full grown 17 year old young man but the first pictures that were circulated were school photos from when he was 11 years old!

Now some may make the claim that this is just how the system is *supposed* to work. That we have an "adversarial" system and that justice is served when the two sides dig their respective heals in and do everything they can to win.

Well, certainly a defense attorney should loyally (but legally) defend their client whole-souled since the defendants are the ones paying them. Also, when we have one little individual against an entire government we need defense attorneys keeping the prosecutors honest as much as possible. That said the prosecution should be out for the truth! They are already much more powerful than the individual defendants and they are supposed to serve the interests of "the people" suggesting a higher calling than simple win statistics. We should want to live in a society where the prosecution is winning when (and only when) all the facts are out in the open. That should be the whole purpose of prosecutors, to fight to get all the facts of the case out in the open and before the jury so that we can all sleep at night knowing that those convicted (ie. those stripped of their liberty) weren't convicted because some dirty prosecutorial trick was played to warp the public's mind, contaminate the jury pool, or twist the facts before the actual jury.

The reality is that this idealistic perception of the role of the prosecutors will never become a reality. So **When Prosecutors Attack** we as jurors need to hold their case to a very high bar. At least a quarter of the time (as in the early 1970's) we need to send the prosecution walking away empty handed. When the police, prosecutors and even judges (in other words all those on the government dole) fail to objectively hand out justice it is left to the **Jury of your peers, thankfully, to keep the state's wrath from indiscriminately falling on the accused.**

Thankfully that is exactly what happened in all three cases here. All three juries executed their duty honorably. In ignorance these juries come under attack, especially the OJ Simpson jury for making up their minds based on race. Anyone making that claim is ignoring a vital fact about how juries function. A jury is not a democracy. The founders did not want people to be imprisoned or executed by mob majority. No, convictions and outright acquittals need to be unanimous in criminal cases (otherwise there is a hung jury). So it didn't matter how racially motivated the 9 black or partially black jurors in the OJ Simpson case were (even though they really were not as you can tell by their interviews) because the three white jurors needed to agree (and of course they did).

In actuality the deciding factor in that Simpson Jury's decision was

NOT race but the fact that **they had been sequestered** away from the poisonous propaganda of the mainstream media. During the case there was a lot of talk about if the jurors were Women first and Black second or vice versa (since most of the jurors were women). In actuality, we have to come to grips with the fact that we are media led drones first and after that come our race and gender identifications. In fact the jury in the civil trial that ruled *against* OJ was in fact made up of jurors that had **consumed countless hours of slanted media coverage** which I believe played a much larger role than their race.

We forget too often that the jurors are by definition the only disinterested objective participants in any trial. Since they don't work for the state or as is the case with judges face elections or political appointments they can be objective (especially when they are kept from the slanted media coverage).

In the George Zimmerman case (like in the OJ Simpson case) the jury was of mixed race (although predominantly white) and reached really the only verdict that could be reached given the facts of the case. It's strange to see the reaction to that verdict. Before Zimmerman was arrested there was lot's of talk about 'letting the system play itself out'. The Martin supporters were saying 'just arrest him. If they just arrested him and charged him and let the facts come out at trial – that's all anyone is asking for.' In reality there were enough facts in front of the police so that they didn't even want to arrest Zimmerman because who could possibly prove he wasn't defending himself when he was badly bruised and Martin had no bruises or wounds besides the mortal shot.

Now what I would like to do is largely put these other cases aside and in the next few chapters focus on the OJ Simpson trial. I'm sure you can appreciate why I felt the need to first deal with the subjects of race and discuss the basic similarities and differences between these cases. If you are watching the news or reading the blogosphere you can see that anyone that attempts to compare the Zimmerman case to OJ, Roderick or pretty much any other case is being branded a racist. I hope by now we have put all that aside and can discuss the vitals of the OJ Simpson criminal trial without all that extra baggage.

# **OJ SIMPSON**: PROSECUTORS ATTACK WITH BROKEN RULES

The first question I always have in investigating a high profile case is this: were standard procedures followed?

Seems like a simple question but the fact is that usually in high-profile cases the first thing that goes out the window is standard procedures. In our culture we hear a lot about thinking "outside the box" and certainly much of the innovation our technological age enjoys comes from thinking about something in a fresh new way. That said a criminal investigation is not the same thing as developing a cutting edge microprocessor. It is more analogous to a consulting project which is an area I know much about. I've spent nearly two decades as a consultant for various government agencies and the projects that always have the most problems are when our standard processes are not followed.

Standard police and prosecutorial procedures may seem dry, and at times arbitrary, but in actuality they are there for a reason and lives can be turned upside-down when they are not followed.

## What Police Procedures?

In the OJ Simpson case practically every rule in the book was thrown out of the window. Before we even get to the prosecutors let's just focus on the police for a moment. Besides any malicious intent, this was partially due to crowd control; there were simply too many cops (and unauthorized personnel) at each crime scene. If you live in what is considered a nice or rich neighborhood have you ever seen what happens when someone calls in a simple robbery in progress? On my block this just happened two weeks ago and within 90 seconds there was a cop outside my neighbor's house. Within 7 minutes our block was filled with police cars as if responding to a small scale invasion from a Central American republic. I mean they would have had decent battle odds against the entire Luxembourg Army. And this was over an anonymous robbery of a middle class house. In our county we even see two, three, and sometimes four cop cars flashing their lights behind a single civilian sedan with one driver pulled over on a traffic violation. Can you imagine the swarm of cops that inundated the crime scenes of what turned out to be the Trial of the Century?

On the morning after the stabbing deaths, the lead detectives arrived at Bundy between 4 and 4:30 AM and by the time they had arrived 18 other non-criminalists and non-coroners had already signed into the crime scene. See, only criminalists were sanctioned to collect evidence and only the coroners could move the body, leaving these other **18 individuals just milling around** observing, securing the premises perhaps and (as later uncovered by OJ's defense team) they were unknowingly destroying footprint evidence (they said they didn't step in visible footprints and by doing so they exposed an embarrassing ignorance for a cop of the fact that many footprints are not visible to the naked eye).

**The next major gaffe** was also likely not due to any malicious intent but nonetheless contaminated the crime scene and that is the fact that the detectives went into her condo, took a blanket from there and laid it on Nicole's body! Now they said this was "to protect Nicole's body from the prying lenses of telescopic cameras, and also to protect the evidence on her corpse, Lange arranged for it to be covered by a blanket from inside the house".

For obvious reasons you simply do not do this. It is standard procedure not to cover any evidence in these situations because trace material from the cover can transfer to the evidence *(and in some cases vital fibers from the body can get picked up when the cover is removed and disposed of).* If something absolutely needs to be covered then a new standard issue clean sheet would be used. This was especially damning in this case because OJ was regularly invited into the condo where he would play games of Monopoly with his kids and what not. So any hairs of his at Bundy must be dismissed as meaningless in this light.

## Police Obviously Planted Blood

Then we start to examine what was done with **blood** in this case. Normally when blood drops are collected they are rehydrated with a moist swab, the swab is then put in a sealed plastic bag and put in a cooler. The reason it is put in a cooler is because if it is not then bacteria can grow within the sample and bacterium does two deleterious things to blood samples. First, it can destroy DNA evidence which is a problem for the police and prosecution (but would not implicate an innocent man). The second thing bacteria do to a blood sample requires a little more explanation. Put simply it **opens the sample up to easily be contaminated**. The DNA of the bacteria and more importantly DNA from microscopic so-called **"blood dust" in a lab can become incorporated into the sample**.

So, were the swatches of blood from Bundy put into a cooler or some other form of refrigeration? No, in fact during this warm California summer day the samples were all stored in the back of an LAPD Criminalistics Laboratory Scene Processing Unit (an ambulance looking vehicle) but the samples were not put in coolers or in any other way refrigerated. This alone would cast doubt on these samples but when you add to it the fact that there was a massive amount of cross contamination between crime scenes and the defense was able to uncover multiple questionable lab practices you have to start doubting any DNA results.

Also, some of the blood was not found until weeks after the murders as was the case with a drop of OJ Simpson's blood on the gate near her condo. Now starting with the weakest point here it should be noted that OJ Simpson was at the "crime scene" not once but repeatedly. His kids lived there and were actually upstairs at the time of the murder. If you have relatives that live close by, say within 5 – 10 minutes' drive, that you visit frequently ask yourself: if an entire police force was combining every inch of their houses, walkways and surrounding area would they find any of your hair fibers? Would they find any of your DNA in the form of sweat, saliva and perhaps blood? It is worth asking but it doesn't end there.

The blood found was laden with EDTA a preservative found in the blood vials like the one that was used to take 8 mL of Simpson's blood (and that was later found with 1.5 mL missing). Now there may have been slightly less of the preservative than would be expected[2] but more importantly there is simply no other way to explain this other than that the blood had been planted. Supporting that conclusion further, the drops suspected to have come from the killer(s) or their knife were sampled; the trainee who collected these samples testified that she put her initials on the coin envelope that contained the samples. Out of all these envelopes the one without her initials is the one that happened to have the EDTA-laden blood that matched with OJ's.

There was some rumblings about the fact that McDonalds (where OJ Simpson ate the night of the murders) uses this preservative in some of their sauces but subsequent experimentation was conducted to show that this would have effectively no change to the level in your blood. The substance appears to breakdown to undetectable levels when digested. Expressing his frustration on this point notice the scary logic used by lead prosecutor **Bill Hodgman**:

> *"I saw* ***nothing to suggest the reality of an LAPD conspiracy****, so with that* ***premise*** *then the effort becomes how do we reconcile the presence of ETDA with the known results. Perhaps the ETDA came from another source… I have to speculate about that. Intuitively* ***I know there is a way to reconcile it, I simply can't explain what it is****".* (emphasis ours)

After a nine month trial, multiple labs, and the endless resources the state threw at this case the man simply cannot reconcile why the blood has this preservative. Can you? It seems very easy for me to reconcile because being a critical thinker means that you are always questioning every premise. I must admit that I came to the OJ Simpson

[2] Although the defense called a witness that suggested the ETDA levels may have started to break down in the sun.

case with the assumption that the police were honorable and would not plant evidence on a suspect. I came from a good neighborhood and had absolutely no reason to question the police, their motives or their findings. But so what? Just because you trust someone or something does not mean that you turn your brain off when evidence that the trust you had has been breached.

## Securing the False Premises

This brings me to another common denominator that you see **When Prosecutors Attack**, namely that they **cling to their "premise"** no matter what especially on high profile cases where they have an extra incentive not to drop the charges when the evidence starts to come up fabricated. I mean as a prosecutor you really have to start with the premise that the police are trustworthy and that the evidence in your case is trustworthy (or else why are you a prosecutor). However, when evidence that questions your premise arises you don't simply dismiss it. You don't say to yourself *"there is no evidence of an LAPD conspiracy so this blood preservative that could not have come from OJ Simpson must have come from some other magical place… the glove was found with a warrantless search by a cop that said he would plant evidence and pleads the fifth when he is asked if he did in fact plant evidence in this case… but that's just the sleazy defense lawyers playing the race card."*

I mean at some point you have to have some respect for critical thinking, for the scientific method and for questioning your premise when the facts demand it. Remember that your "premise" is not itself evidence, in fact it is supposed to be the *result* of evidence. Instead, Hodgman says "I saw nothing to suggest the reality of an LAPD conspiracy" to implicate Simpson **right as he dismisses such evidence**! It is only the unreality created by the media that has left the public with the impression that the questioning of lab preservative was a dirty defense lawyer trick when in fact **the exact opposite is true**. This was a dirty trick of the LAPD that the prosecution tried to push through. Had the defendant been some random punk this planted evidence would have just appeared like a DNA match to the jury and the man would be in jail.

But even without all this fancy fangled science babble you could have proved that OJ's blood must have been planted at the crime scene and this bold statement can be made because OJ Simpson had absolutely no cuts that could have left any of his own blood. Now I know your brain must be hurting because the media has told you that he had a "gash" on his middle finger that police noticed the next day when he got back from Chicago. While it is true that OJ had a cut on his middle finger when he came back from Chicago it is an absolute lie to say that he had this cut on the way to Chicago. Why can I say it is categorically untrue that OJ had a cut on his middle finger before arriving in Chicago? Well, without going into a Sermon many of us intuitively accept the Judeo-Christian concept of two witnesses establishing something as being credible. Regardless of our background we all intuitively accept that multiple corroborating witnesses have more evidentiary value than a single person's claim in a criminal case.

In this case we have **10 (as in TEN) witnesses to establish that he had no cuts on his hands** on the way to Chicago and **exactly zero that claim otherwise**. Also, these were not just witnesses for the defense but as our friends at Wikipedia put it *"both prosecution and defense witnesses testified to not seeing any cuts or wounds of any kind on Simpson's hands in the hours after the murders took place"*.

Did these witnesses just not notice either way so maybe they just overlooked a cut on someone else's hand? No, interestingly they have **positive memories** of there being no cuts. If I had a cut and was traveling I'm sure no one would care or notice but I am not a sports legend/movie star that is regularly being asked for my autograph (although I challenge anyone to beat me at a game of foosball – which yes *is a sport*).

His limo driver, Allan Park, was not his regular driver and had looked forward to meeting Simpson. He testified that he shook his hand: **no blood, no Band-Aids or cuts**.

Jim Merrill, who was a Hertz corporate sales representative who picked Simpson up at the Chicago airport, described him as friendly and relaxed, even greeting those who approached him in the airport. He saw him sign some papers: **no blood, no Band-Aids or cuts**.

Stephen Valerie, a UCLA student recognized Simpson and stated, "He was very pleasant, smiling. I noted his clothing was very well pressed. He looked sharp". More importantly he was sitting near OJ the entire flight and he said he examined Simpson's fingers because he was hoping to see a Super Bowl ring (of course OJ never received a Super Bowl ring but he didn't know that). More to the point: **no blood, no Band-Aids or cuts**.

Then there was Wayne Stanfield. Now you know you are famous when the pilot comes out to see you and that's just what happened during the American Airlines flight to Chicago. He shook Mr. Simpson's hand and said he had a firm handshake and that nothing seemed to be physically wrong with him. Again: **no blood, no Band-Aids or cuts**. Also, he spent hours on this plane to Chicago and they scoured it looking for any of OJ's blood and they did not find a drop or even a spec of it.

Besides this there were multiple people that testified that he was signing pictures for them and if you have ever had a celebrity sign something you know that you are watching their hands as they bestow their John Hancock on your forever-to-be-treasured memento. All of them say basically the same thing: **no blood, no Band-Aids or cuts**.

If needed they could have produced an additional ten witnesses to confirm that there was no signs of his hands having any cuts but there was simply no need. The prosecution could not find a single witness to the cuts until his trip back from Chicago. **Ten witnesses versus zero** is really tantamount to **establishing this as a fact**.

Oh and in case you were wondering if the blood could have come from some other cut on OJ's body that is simply not possible. Upon Mr. Simpson's return to LA he submitted himself to a physical examination and the only cut on his whole body was the cut on his middle finger which we now know simply did not exist on his egress from California on the night of the murders. This is the sort of exculpatory evidence that would bring an honest, self-aware, prosecutor to file a motion to dismiss the charges against the defendant. He could not have left any blood at the scene and the blood they do find contains a lab preservative. Okay, we thought we had the right guy and the police seemed to have helped that conclusion along a little to make their job easier but now we need to drop the idea that OJ committed these crimes and either release him unless you can now establish that someone did this in his behalf (which would require evidence of such communication and/or payment that simply did not exist).

Before moving on we need to come to grips with the fact that OJ Simpson's **lack of bruises and cuts** should at a minimum prove that he was not one of the actual killers (yes there were multiple we will get to that later). How can I say this? Well, we have to go back to the initial autopsy and coroner reports. There is a lot in there that makes it difficult for the prosecution's case. The coroner's report states that Nicole last spoke with her mother at around 11 pm when OJ was already in his limo on the way to the airport (but we will get to the timeline later). More to the point the autopsy reports on both Nicole and Ron show extensive defensive wounds. In other words they were both fighting for their life. Ron was covered with defensive wounds more than Nicole but it should be noted that some of her wounds were on her hands suggesting that they were "active" rather than "passive" defensive wounds as if she had time to try and grab the knife from the assailant (of course unsuccessfully).

There are some misleading re-enactments online that show the both of them being murdered within 5 or 10 seconds and this is extremely misleading. The wounds show that there was a protracted struggle and most experts agree that the assailant would at a minimum have bruises and one expert said they would expect bruises, a broken nose or even a couple of broken ribs.

The idea that someone (OJ or otherwise) could have inflicted not just the fatal wounds but the defensive wounds with not so much as a bruise or cut on them is implausible. Ten undisputed witnesses attest to the fact that OJ Simpson had no cuts on his hands on the way to Chicago (some of them adding that they specifically studied his hands). The physical examination confirmed he had no other marks other than the cut he received while away in Chicago.

If your mind is not open but bent towards the inevitable conclusion that the prosecution just must be right then it starts to warp your ability to think clearly. One great example of this is when defenders of the state discuss the presence of lab preservative on Nicole's blood that appeared on OJ's socks they "found"[3] in the middle of his bedroom floor. Any rational person should accept that if you test blood on a sock and it already has preservative on it that it was planted. But notice how how Thomas L. Jones puts it in his article "The Murder Trial of O.J. Simpson":

> *Dr. Cotton from Cellmark had also testified regarding EDTA used to stop the degradation of blood. When she had checked the autopsy blood taken from Nicole, she had found that it was more degraded than her matching blood found*

[3] I put the word "found" in quotes because the police made a video of every room in OJ's house the day after the killings and the room (where the socks were found weeks later) was shown to have no socks which only makes sense if they were planted later on by someone that was unaware of the police video tape or who forgot that they had documented each room. Below is a still from the video showing indeed no socks weeks before they were "found":

> *on the sock in the bedroom. Once blood has degraded, it is impossible to raise its DNA count. Under the defense's conspiracy theory, the blood on the sock* **had to have come from Nicole's autopsy vial***, but this blood had a lower DNA count than her blood on the sock. In other words, it was fresher when it splashed onto Simpson's sock as he was killing her, than it was* **two days later** *when the coroner collected it. It is impossible for degraded blood to become fresh again, proving that Nicole's blood on the sock could not have been planted.* (Emphasis ours)

I hope you can follow his convoluted logic so that I can jump right to explaining the false conclusion. Remember, that there was plenty of Nicole's blood on the scene – no one was keeping track of the quantity of her blood on the scene. The only blood that was finite and tracked was from OJ because he voluntarily donated 8 mL and they "lost" 1.5 mL of it (*and all the blood they found of OJ in the field amounts to much less than the 1.5 mL discrepancy*). In the above excerpt Jones makes the same false assumption that most pro-prosecution drones make in connection with Nicole's blood on the sock and that assumption is that Nicole's blood could only come from two places: the autopsy vial OR from it freshly pouring out at the time of the killing. This is a dangerous assumption because in his own comments he concedes that **the coroner takes her blood two days later**. In that time multiple authorized and unauthorized personnel from the LAPD are coming and going from the crime scene so *who knows* how much of Nicole's blood was collected in that time. The point is that any blood collected in that time frame would have "fresher" DNA than what was collected by the coroner AND it would have the EDTA preservative (which cannot be said of the blood spilling out of Nicole at the time of the murder).

Regardless of what the prosecution tried to say after EDTA was found in OJ's blood at the gate and Nicole's blood on his sock, EDTA simply does not show up in detectable levels unless it is coming from a criminalists vial (although the inverse is not necessarily true – the absence of EDTA is not proof that blood wasn't planted). Remember that when the defense started to make rumblings about evidence being planted it was Marcia Clark that sent it to be tested for the presence of EDTA so that she could prove that it wasn't planted (or at least wasn't planted from blood that came from a "purple top vial") and then when she didn't get the result she wanted she tried to explain that it didn't prove anything. This type of duplicity really gets under my skin. Before the state sends any evidence to be tested they should have to commit to the conclusion that should be made if the test is negative and if the test is positive. Otherwise the test becomes meaningless because it can mean anything the state wants it to mean. Thankfully this duplicity was not missed by the Jury.

## The Frame Fit Like a Glove

As I've said the jury didn't care about the gloves not fitting (in fact they came out and said they dismissed that demonstration out of hand) but they simply were not going to swallow some ludicrous alternate-universe theory where it makes sense for blood stains to contain preservative and not be planted. If only that fair minded multi-racial, multi-gendered educated jury had the last word and OJ was still a free man (and let's not pretend for one minute that the Las Vegas "kidnapping" case non-sense wasn't payback for this acquittal).

So this should cover OJ's blood at the scene of the crime (aka. South Bundy) and Nicole's blood on his miraculously re-appearing socks but what about Nicole and Ron's blood in the infamous Bronco? Before I answer that I want to express my frustration with this pile of phony evidence we have to deal with when we are in OJ's camp. The only thing I can compare it to is if you were living in Nazi Germany and having to explain away every attack leveled against the Jews. Yes, I went there and for good reason. Imagine that we are really in 1938 Germany and at a dinner party. Someone says some absurd racist statement (like that the Jews sacrifice children during Passover which was circulated in Nazi literature) about Jews that you begin to refute. Half way through someone else jumps in with "*come on, it's right there in The Protocols of the Elders of Zion...*" (a fake document created by an anti-Semite in the middle ages) and a third person jumps and makes reference to some other repeated lie they have heard repeated so many times on German television that it just must be true. By the end of the night you are frustrated, you haven't changed anyone's mind and likely the next morning the gestapo will be knocking on your door to take you away. This really isn't too far off when being put in the position to refute piece after piece of **fabricated or contaminated evidence**.

That said, let's get back to the Bronco and start with the fact that there is a very small amount of combined blood in the Bronco (so it could all fit in a thimble for example and all the blood that wasn't OJ's could fit on the head of a thumb tact); remember the prosecutions story is that OJ jumped in the Bronco dripping in the blood of the slain which is just not consistent with the nearly microscopic specs found in the Bronco. I mean in greyscale it is hardly noticeable as in the following figure:

***Figure 5:*** *Tiny Specs of Blood Transferred From Crime Scene*

## The Dog Ate All My Credible Evidence

Even so, where did these specs of blood come from? What would be more consistent with the tiny specs of blood transfer? This is a bit of a long story so let me just give you the short answer first: they went from the crime scene → to a dog (Akita) → to animal control officer → Bronco. There may have been other evidence transfers of a more malicious nature *(and the animal control officer wasn't the only unauthorized person to be in the Bronco prior to the blood collection)* but there is solid reason to believe that this evidence was the result of sheer sloppiness and disregard for protocol.

So, here is the long version. For reasons unknown the door to Nicole Brown's condo was left ajar after the killings and her dog Kato (an Akita) was out and about pacing back and forth distraughtly (poor dog) and as a result its paws and underbelly had soaked up so much blood the dog's hair was referred to as being "matted in red".

Just before 11:00, Steven Schwab, who was walking his own dog, came across the distressed dog (Kato). It followed him home where he then noticed the blood on the dog. Schwab then asked his neighbor, Suka Boztepe, to take care of the animal overnight. Mr. Boztepe agreed, but afterward the dog was persistently restless, so Boztepe and his partner, Bettina Rasmussen, decided to walk the dog and try and calm it down. The dog dragged them back to number 875, where the Akita stopped and gazed down a dim, tree-shaded pathway. Following the dog's stare, they saw a shape of someone lying at the foot of some steps and part of the body sprawled under the iron fence.

So we can see how important this dog was in getting the ball rolling with the police since they were, of course, called once the bodies were discovered. But what happened to this faithful canine? Well, the LAPD eventually sent Sergeant Donn Yarnell of the animal-control unit to examine the Akita. They were trying to categorize the dog as either aggressive or passive to see if it would have attacked its owner's attackers[4] (they determined that the dog was **overly passive and would not have**). The strange part of the story is that the animal-control officer ends up in the Bronco after spending time with an Akita "matted" in blood from the crime scene.

There is also evidence that the infamous Mark Fuhrman was in the Bronco and he was of course at the South Bundy crime scene where he found one (or more likely two) glove(s). The following is a picture of Mark Furhman at Bundy practically in a pool of blood before he goes to Rockingham (OJ's home) and we will show that he was in the Bronco as well:

---

[4] Their testing likely mimicked the American Kennel Club's CGC (or Canine Good Citizen) Test in which a dog is tested to see how the dog in question would react to a sudden distraction. Animal Control would also want to see how the dog would react to an unexpected scenario by shocking the dog with something outside its normal frame of reference (like banging a shovel against a wheel barrel) according to certified Service Dog Trainer we consulted while investigating for this book.

The Bundy crime scene: Mark Fuhrman pointing to the single glove.

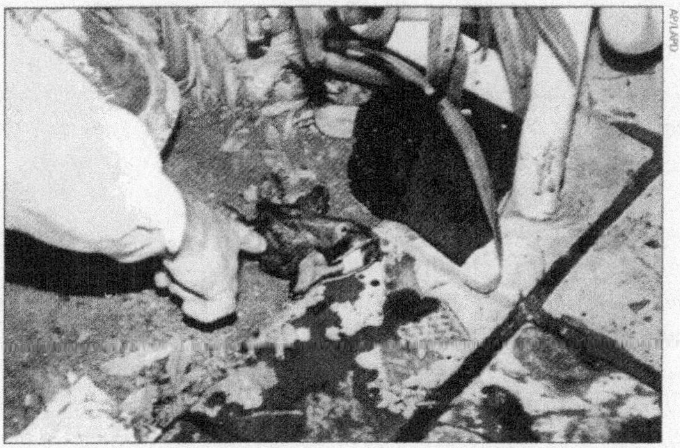


A closeup of the same glove and the black knit cap (note the distinctive heel impression in foreground).

***Figure 6:*** *Fuhrman at Bundy Among Pool of Victims Blood*

Now we will get into how we know that Mark Fuhrman was in the Bronco (*even though he makes the impossible claim that the Bronco was locked*) but I'm sure you can appreciate the very real contamination threat inherent when an officer goes directly from the above crime scene to

Mr. Simpson's home and in his Bronco. Oh, and did I mention Mark Fuhrman's shoe size? The racist cop has a size 12 which easily explains a partial bloody shoe impression that was consistent with OJ's shoe size which was the same as Fuhrman's. Of course, it doesn't end there so I would like you to consider a more complete summation of the small amount of blood in the Bronco made by William C. Thompson, Professor, Department of Criminology, Law & Society, University of California, Irvine, California. Thompson was a legal contributor to the defense team and had this to say:

> *The defense offered several explanations for the presence of DNA consistent with the victims' in the Bronco.* ***One possibility****, the defense argued, is that the victims'* ***blood was planted*** *in the Bronco by detective Mark Fuhrman in order to frame Simpson. Under this theory, Fuhrman swiped the Rockingham glove inside the Bronco in order to plant the victims' blood there. Although the detectives testified that the Bronco was locked when they first saw it and denied that anyone had opened the doors while it was at Simpson's residence, the defense pointed to evidence suggesting that Fuhrman had, in fact, opened the door of the Bronco. In his testimony, Fuhrman reported seeing blood stains on the lower sill of the Bronco's door. Photographs of the Bronco showed that there were indeed stains where Fuhrman reported them, but* ***they could be seen only when the door of the Bronco was open****.*
>
> *Even if Fuhrman did not swipe the glove in the Bronco, he* ***might have transferred the victims' DNA there unintentionally****, the defense argued. A photo taken at the crime scene showed* ***Fuhrman standing in a pool of the victims' blood*** *pointing at a glove. It was after this photo was taken that* ***Fuhrman went with the other detectives to Rockingham****. If Fuhrman then entered the Bronco looking for evidence, the defense argued, the blood consistent with Nicole Simpson on the carpet could have come from Fuhrman's shoe. Fuhrman or another officer who had a bit of the victims' blood on a sleeve or shirt cuff could have accidentally swiped it onto the Bronco console while exploring for evidence.*
>
> *A third explanation is that the victims' blood was* ***planted in the Bronco while it was at a storage facility****. On June 14, 1994, Dennis Fung first collected blood from the Bronco. The defense established that it was a general practice of criminalists, when swabbing blood, to collect the entire*

*sample.* ***Three witnesses testified*** *that they had been in the Bronco after June 14 and* ***saw no blood.*** *On August 26, 1994, the Bronco was again inspected and blood was found on the console* ***in the same location where Fung had collected the initial samples.*** *In the interim, the Bronco was left at an unsecured storage facility where a large number of people had access to it and unauthorized persons were known to have entered it looking for souvenirs. Finally, the defense argued that there could have been tampering with the Bronco swatches in the LAPD crime laboratory. If Nicole Brown Simpson's blood was planted on the sock, then her blood and that of Ronald Goldman could have been planted in the Bronco swatches as well.* [5] (**bolding** and italics ours)

So as far as broken rules are concerned Thompson touches on multiple touch points where procedure was thrown out the window and how these aren't technicalities that a defendant can "get off on" (a term the media loves to repeat) but in fact are protocols that when not followed leaves misleading evidence to appear that cannot be explained by anything besides contamination or malicious planting.

The last paragraph I quoted from Dr. Thompson makes a great but unsettling point that on August 26th, 1994 they inspect an area that Dennis Fung **already collected** samples from and produced **new evidence!** This reminds me of what Josef Stalin said about the electoral process (loosely translated): "It's **not** the people who vote that count. It's **the people who count the votes**".

I suppose if Stalin were alive today he might say of the evidentiary process in America that 'it's not the evidence that determines what is collected. It's the collectors that determine the evidence'.

Similarly, in "Gangs of New York" the quasi-historical character Boss Tweed said during election day: "Remember the first rule of politics. The ballots don't make the results, **the counters make the results**. The counters. Keep counting."

Again, if they didn't like the evidence collected by Dennis Fung, just send someone else in and tell them to "keep counting"... I mean "keep looking". Right.

---

[5] Citation: William C. Thompson, DNA Evidence in the O.J. Simpson Trial, Colorado Law Review, 67 (4), 827-857 (1996)

*Figure 7: LAPD Contaminates Evidence Sent to Labs*

Unfortunately, this is not an exhaustive coverage of the police mishaps and misdeeds in this case; not even close. One area I've really gone light on is the mishaps in the LAPD lab. There were so many procedures in the lab that were disregarded to the detriment of the lab's credibility and the credibility of the evidence it produced. Remember, they don't really find "OJ's blood" at such and such location instead they find something they think is blood, collect it, and send it to a lab with a bunch of other evidence and someone in that lab tests it and IF the evidence wasn't contaminated and IF the evidence didn't get mislabeled and IF the evidence was stored properly so it didn't rub up against reference samples IF the chain of custody was clearly established and so on… in other words if you get past all the IF's then you can have reliable evidence that you can use to take someone's liberty away when eyewitnesses and smoking guns are not available. Did we pass through all these IF's for enough of the evidence to make any sort of believable case against Simpson? Hardly!

In fact, here is just a couple of more examples where the IF's broke down. First, we have criminalist Susan Brockbank who admitted on the stand that the two gloves, a cap found near the crime scene and a piece of carpet from Simpson's Bronco were all **stored in the same box** at the crime lab. They may have been in separate bags but this is still extremely unwise since even microscopic "blood dust" can be transferred through bags that are not completely sealed. This would be less of an issue had the blood taken been properly cooled after being collected.

Inside and outside of the lab there were egregious errors made. Henry Lee, director of Connecticut State Forensics Science Laboratory, testified during the trial that they found a trail of seven blood drops leading away from the killing scene but these drops and the blood on Ms. Simpson's back was never collected for analysis by police chemists who made "terrible" errors handling evidence. Of course, it's possible they didn't feel the pressure at the time since they could always go back and "find" the suspects artificially preserved blood on the gate thanks to a little help from their friend EDTA.

I joke about that point but the reality is that the Rampart scandal revealed that widespread planting of inculpatory evidence, the covering up of exculpatory evidence, police engaging in perjury, and the deliberate framing of suspects was commonplace within the LAPD (although the media desperately scrambled to try and characterize this as a problem exclusive to their CRASH anti-gang unit). Again, a widespread investigation should have immediately ensued as a result of the OJ Simpson trial alone. Even if you were still in the Prosecution's camp you simple cannot escape that some of the evidence was planted. The blood on the gate and the blood on the socks should be enough to at least convince you that they tried to "frame a guilty man" as some have said. The fact that they framed an innocent man should have put every case in the LAPD under immediate scrutiny. I mean how many cases were there that put defendants with shallow pockets away with EDTA laden DNA evidence? Part of me doesn't even want to know but we will get into that a bit more later. For now let's switch focus squarely on the prosecution for a moment and give our boy's in blue a little break.

## Prosecutors, Persecutors and Outright Clowns

Trust is a very strange substance. **Trust, when you have it, is as strong as steel**. It is the fabric of sturdy relationships of all varieties. Yet, when someone violates that trust the steal like strength evaporates and it crumbles like the proverbial cookie.

How is trust supposed to function in a courtroom? Well, the Jury is supposed to trust that the prosecution is the good guys out for truth, justice and so forth. They also trust that the defense attorney's will do everything in their power to advocate for their client. Unlike the prosecution that – at any moment that it appears to be appropriate – can file a motion to drop the charges, a defense lawyer can't simply file a motion to end the trial with a guilty verdict simply because he realizes that his client is guilty. The prosecutor should only have one reason for everything they say and do and that is because it is the truth. A defendants innocence is likely a huge motivator for a defense attorney but even when such innocence is non-existent the lawyer is still ethically obligated (and monetarily motivated) to continue in his advocacy.

So by their very nature the prosecution is supposed to be more trustworthy from a juror's perspective. In effect, since the prosecutor is representing "the people" they are serving the Jury who are members of "the people" and who don't want to live in a community with murders and such on the loose.

The prosecution in the OJ Simpson case violated the public's trust at every turn. We'll get to the tricks they tried to pull on the Jury in a moment but first let's examine the number they tried to pull on the general public. First, we already discussed that they **released a phony photo** to make the public think that OJ was abusive and hit her (which he never did). The photo found in **Figure** was of course made on a movie set and the prosecution leaks it to the press anyway. Truth is unimportant as long as it helps their case.

Next, they start playing with words. If you were old enough to be watching the news on the day that OJ Simpson was arrested then you witnessed a monolithic deception from the mainstream media. This deception is with regard to the F-word. Not the one you are thinking about. **They called OJ Simpson a fugitive**. Before we explain this let's look at what the legal definition of a "fugitive" is and then we can determine if this applies to OJ's situation:

*"a person convicted or accused of a crime who hides from law enforcement in the state or flees across state lines to avoid arrest or punishment."*

The problem with applying this definition to OJ Simpson is that Simpson had arrangements later that day to meet police at the station when they made the announcement that they were going to take him into custody. He was hardly "hiding" nor did he make any attempt to cross state lines. Now he did have a sizable amount of cash on him but remember we are talking about a multi-millionaire not some drug dealer. He was not a fugitive and regardless of what he may of thought of doing he was simply driving around and went back home to possibly see his kids one more time before being taken into custody.

There was no high speed chase or any resisting of arrest going on here. Instead we have manipulation; **we have police and prosecutors engaging in a stunt** to make OJ Simpson look guilty in the eyes of the public. They could have simply taken him into custody during his appointment with them later that day. For that matter they had multiple opportunities to arrest him before that day since he was in fact co-operating with police as far as he possibly could.

The stunts didn't stop there. The preliminary hearing alone should have been enough to show that there was something wrong with the prosecution's case. Had the defense not requested a bench decision instead of being decided by a grand jury this case might have never gone to trial. One of the strangest aspects of the preliminary hearing was the justification the police and prosecution offered for why a search was conducted without a warrant. For those unfamiliar with the Fourth Amendment it protects us all against "unreasonable" searches and then essentially defines reasonable as having received a specific (stating where is being searched and what is being searched for) warrant based on probable cause.

No warrant was obtained before police illegally entered Rockingham (OJ's house) and Mark Fuhrman "discovered" the glove. So how did this piece of "evidence" make it into the trial? Why wasn't it summarily dismissed as "fruit from the poisonous tree" as it should have been? Good question. There is no good answer to that but what I can tell you is the ludicrous story the police and prosecution tried to hoist on us all. See, while a warrant is required (per the Constitution) there are so-called exigent circumstances that the Supreme Court has long ruled allow for exceptions to be made. The most commonly used example to illustrate this is if a police officer hears someone inside a building yell "Help me!" at the top of their lungs the officer doesn't need to wake up a judge in the middle of the night and wait for him to issue a warrant before going in to help the citizen in distress. While this exception is not noted in the Constitution this is a concession that was long made by the courts. So, did the late Vannatter (the lead investigator) hear some damsel in distress screaming for help? No, he doesn't even try to make that claim. Did he have knowledge or evidence of anyone in the house being injured or in need of medical attention? Not even close. Was Rockingham on fire with an empty school bus parked outside suggesting a bunch of school children were in trouble? No, not that either. Then what was it that provided him with the evidence that there were sufficient exigent circumstances to step over Mr. Simpson's 4th amendment rights? Well, take a look at the following figure and let me know if you think there is anything in this picture that tells us there was some dire emergency in progress at Rockingham on the night of this unwarranted search:

***Figure 8:*** *Parked Erratically?*

So do you see the clear evidence of an emergency inside the house? No? What's that, you only see a white Bronco that's been parallel parked? Well, that is what I see as well. Vannatter instead claimed that the Bronco was "parked at an angle" and "with the rear end *jutting out* into the roadway".

Does the Bronco look like it's jutting out into the roadway to you? True it is parked at a miniscule angle (roughly a 2 degree angle) but if this is "exigent" circumstances then that would give police the right to enter and search practically any premises with a car parked in front of it. The fact that Judge Ito made the unconscionable decision to allow the resulting "evidence" into the trial has to go down as his biggest gaffe of the trial (although again this is a mistake that carried over from pretrial).

Of course the officer that "found" the resulting poisonous fruit had to eventually plead the 5$^{th}$ amendment when asked if he had planted evidence in this case so in the minds of the jurors this "evidence" had been effectively neutralized (so no harm, no foul I suppose). Keep in mind that while this reckless disregard for the fourth amendment was initially perpetrated by the LAPD the fact remains that the prosecution included this in their justification to include the evidence that caused this to go to trial. If the prosecution wasn't on the attack regardless of truth and justice they would not have presented this as legitimate exigent circumstances.

As if that were not enough, the prosecution knowingly withheld evidence in an attempt to concoct a fabricated picture of OJ Simpson's demeanor the night of the murders. The prosecution put up two witnesses (one being Nicole's sister) that portrayed OJ as in a dark scowling mood during his daughter's recital that he and the Brown family attended just hours before the gruesome killings.

The problem is that they knew this depiction was completely false. Normally the prosecution loves dumping all the evidence on the defense lawyers. Normally they have such a compelling case and out gun the defense to such a degree that defense lawyers often comment that they are quick to rub their evidence in their noses. Of course nothing can be called normal when it comes to the OJ Simpson trial and the prosecution sat on multiple pieces of exculpatory evidence including a tape that completely contradicted their depiction of OJ being in a dark scowling mood the night of the murders. It later came out that they had possession of this tape but the defense team had to see it air on Hard

Copy before they knew of the tape. Apparently a Mr. Kennedy-Scott was videotaping various aspects of the recital Simpson was attending that night because Simpson's daughter was performing. Kennedy-Scott also had a child participating but when he sees OJ in the parking lot he takes a candid camera of him from a good distance. Even so it is clear from this video that OJ was relaxed and that he had a good relationship with the Brown family. Denise was obviously not afraid of him or at odds with OJ as she affectionately approaches him and kisses him as shown in **Figure** below:

***Figure 9:*** *OJ and Brown Family Harmony*

Try and watch the entire video if you can get your hands on it because the tape establishes that he was in a good mood that night (at the very least while at the recital); it establishes that the Brown family had a warm relationship with him (which we will expound on in a bit) despite the fact that he had divorced Nicole; it establishes that they did not scorn him as some abusive monster and most importantly it shows that the prosecution was not out for truth but were out for a win because they painted a false picture to the jury that evaporated with the release of this amateur video.

Why was there such a warm relationship? Well the truth is that OJ had been taking care of the extended Brown family almost down to the person. Before I expound on this point it is worth mentioning that the Brown parents are never seen saying anything pejorative about OJ Simpson (unlike the Goldman father who has made a career out of demonizing OJ). So let's chronicle all of the good deeds OJ did for this family that he did for no reason other than he was a decent guy with money.

Starting with Nicole's sisters, OJ paid for Dominique to go to college (this is the sister that later sold posed topless pictures of her dead sister to the National Enquirer for $32,500) and he paid for another sister to get elective plastic surgery (aka. a boob job). After the divorce, in spite of having a prenuptial agreement protecting most of OJ's assets Nicole was left with a very nice place for her and their kids to live, a nearly half a million dollar settlement and eventually settling on $10k per month from OJ (which was more than double that for over a year). Not bad when you have no mortgage.

Then there were Nicole's parents. Nicole's father, Louis Brown, ran into financial difficulties at one point and OJ again came to save the day by giving him a large sum that Marcia Clarke tried to call an "investment" during the trial. Let me tell you OJ didn't think he was getting in on the ground floor of the next Microsoft. Even if OJ called it an investment himself that is just what you say when you are trying to help someone save face. To their credit, Louis and Juditha have maintained their dignity through all of this (for the most part) and unlike Denise they have not sought to make money off the death of their daughter. Instead their public comments center around the welfare of their grandchildren which appears to be sincere

Inside the recital his mood also seems to be congenial as pictured in **Figure** but that doesn't stop the prosecution trying to twist the facts. They tried to say that OJ was so upset that he stormed out of the recital shortly after arriving only to return later in a foul mood. The truth of course is that he arrives and in typical dad-fashion didn't think to buy flowers for his daughter but sees all the other parents have flowers. So he gets up and gets the flowers that you can see depicted in the next photo. Could anything be more innocent?

The prosecution effectively lies to the jury and suggests OJ left because he was "simmering" when the obvious truth is that he left to get flowers and his mood is established by **Figure** and **Figure** and remember that while he is posing for the latter he was unaware of the videographer that captured the former[6]. Besides which, even if OJ was "acting" you can't say that the Brown family was acting along with him, can you? Their demeanor shows the simple truth about OJ: namely that he was liked not just by fans but by his ex-wife's family whom he cared for dutifully. Anyone that has been through a divorce or been close to one knows that being warmly embraced by the in-laws post-divorce says a tremendous amount (since in-laws naturally side with the ex-spouse).

Of course **When Prosecutors Attack** they have no qualms about painting a misleading picture and holding onto exculpatory evidence that would interfere with their rouse (as certainly was the case here). In fact, in a shocking 5-4 decision the Supreme Court has just made it easier for District Attorneys and their underlings to knowingly push forward false or misleading evidence by removing any civil liability the office would have for doing so. The Supreme Court's decision in Connick v. Thompson virtually gives license to prosecutors to lie, fabricate or withhold evidence, since they apparently can't be held accountable for knowingly or intentionally sending an innocent man to prison and even death row.

In this case Thompson was convicted of armed robbery in 1985, before he stood trial for the murder of Raymond Liuzza, the son of a prominent New Orleans hotel owner. His ultimate conviction for the murder had him sitting on death row (and at one point Thompson came within weeks of being executed). Fortunately for Thompson a pair of Pennsylvanian lawyers from a large Philadelphia-based law firm took up his case to try and spare him from the death penalty. But in 1999, an investigator discovered that there was a blood test conducted in the armed robbery case that showed that Thompson was not the perpetrator. Prosecutors acknowledged that it was withheld from Thompson's attorneys. Even though this injustice that could have cost his life was not in dispute the Supreme Court found that the DA's office was not liable. In the majority opinion they stated that a single incident is not enough to prove liability and they needed to see a "pattern of

---

[6] Figure 9 comes in a little blurry but you can see this video as part of the defense teams closing arguments in the criminal trial.

similar violations in order to prove liability. What's the opposite of a "chilling effect"? If I was a prosecutor reading their decision I wouldn't be too worried about fabricating evidence. I mean it's really no big deal to knowingly send an innocent man or two to be executed… just – you know – don't go and make a regular practice of it. Fabricate a little evidence here, withhold some exculpatory evidence there, knowingly send a few innocent people to get executed now and then but just don't go overboard. I'm sure every rouge prosecutor is shaking in their boots.

***Figure 10:*** *Relaxed, Happy, Proud Poppa (with flowers)*

So let's get back to the OJ Simpson trial. Even with all of this evidence of prosecutorial abuse you may still have some questions about this case. The most common are "**why** would the state arrest and prosecute an innocent man?" and "if it wasn't OJ **then who did it**?"

Both are kind of unfair loaded questions (like "why would a leader of Germany round up and kill millions of Jews?" it is difficult to answer but it occurred nonetheless) but we will deal with the former and then in the next chapter address the latter. In discussing this try and not project your values onto these prosecutors. Those that seek political office tend to be less scrupulous than the average citizen. Even so I think even the average person would be lured by some of the inducements set before prosecutors and even law enforcement officials on these high profile cases.

### What Would a Prosecutor Have to Gain?

Everything! Let me first say that I don't think Marcia Clark (or any of these prosecutors for that matter) is a particularly bad person. That said she is not a particularly good person either. If you think about it you would have to be a **really excellent person to turn away the lottery ticket** she was given when she was put on this case. Imagine you are her and you get this case. Think of everything she had to do right in her life in order to be in the position to get the case of the century. Think of all the p's and q's she had to mind; think of the pay cut she had to take to take a position in the office of the District Attorney. Why do people become lawyers? Why would someone limit their earning potential to take a position as a prosecutor? There may be some noble sentiments mixed in there (and many just like the stability and benefits associated with working for Uncle Sam) but the cold truth is that these positions have a lot of potential for upward political mobility. That's why you jockey to become a prosecutor, to put some criminals away, score some points with the Law and Order crowd, make some splashy press conferences and seek higher office. Prosecutors frequently move to legislative positions and get sent to congress or take assembly posts; some of them even get elected to executive positions and become Mayor or Governor.

When Marcia Clark became the most visible member of the state's team of prosecutors it really was like winning the lottery. If she prosecuted the trial of the century and won it would surely have secured her a congressional seat and if she had a more stable family life she would have had a reasonable shot of a Governorship. Certainly a senate seat, which is worth tens of millions especially coming from a powerful state like California, would have been in play. As it turned out the consolation prize for losing wasn't half bad either. Marcia Clark received a non-refundable advance of 4.3 million for her lame post-trial book and since she was a well-known public figure she was given a contract as a television correspondent. Since then she has written three additional books and received some acting work. The point here is that either way, win or lose, Marcia Clark's life had changed forever and all she had to do was continue with the trial. In her closing arguments she tried to say that if she felt the evidence wasn't compelling or that the evidence had been planted or tampered with that she could file a motion to dismiss the charges. While this is technically true you have to appreciate that she would have to overcome an intense instinct of self-interest to do so.

So, when you get a case like this the wealth and prominence has to cloud the thinking of all but the most honorable members of our society. Even Mark Fuhrman, a discredited racist cop, was able to finagle speaking engagements, book deals and paid TV appearances. It's ridiculous when people ask "why would a cop plant evidence?" when there is this clear example of how making yourself central to the case of the century benefited him to such a superlative degree. Was there a conspiracy to frame OJ? We will touch on that a bit in the next chapter but it is somewhat beside the point. There doesn't need to be an organized conspiracy when each individual had so much to gain from charging and prosecuting Mr. Simpson. The fact that the media jumps on board only makes it easier to avoid any internal reflection. The media created such hatred against OJ Simpson that you could feel the tension in California after the trial. I remember driving around after the case and seeing billboards depicting OJ with a knife and saying a murderer was out on the loose!

Now as an author I really do not begrudge anyone writing, publishing and profiting from their books, my only point is that the state and the individuals that represent it have a tremendous amount to gain from winning at all costs. This is why we saw repeated prosecutorial misconduct from Ms. Clark and Mr. Darden especially. We saw them hold back exculpatory video's while creating a false impression of OJ's mood with the Jury; we saw the prosecution release phony abuse photos just to curry the public's support; we saw the prosecution send blood evidence to labs to test for the presence of EDTA and then when the results showed the presence of EDTA they tried to tell us the sky was yellow and that its normal to have lab preservative in your blood. Not only that, but we saw the prosecution try and swap out the attending coroner when they didn't like his report that suggests this crime was likely committed by at least two killers.

Along the same lines we saw the police conduct unconstitutional searches on Rockingham; we saw Vanatter under oath stating that the Bronco was "jutting out into the roadway" when your own eyes bear witness that this was a fraudulent lie; we saw Fuhrman perjure himself and then plead the fifth when asked if he "planted" evidence; we saw missing blood from a vile taken from OJ; we saw crooked cops traveling around to the crime scenes with OJ's blood in their pocket; we saw reference samples mixed in with key pieces of evidence and the list goes on and on.

Above all we saw a lot of broken rules and a lot of time when the defense would ask 'have you ever done anything like this in any other case' the law enforcement officials would have to respond with an embarrassing "no".

You know, in the government whenever they use the word "Special" you know you are in trouble. For example if you ever get audited by the IRS you should know that while this is a very unpleasant experience, and however you slice it they usually want some more money out of your pocket, you usually aren't really in trouble unless they introduce you to a "Special" Agent. Then you get up and demand legal/financial representation before answering anymore questions if you know what's good for you.

The same is true of these "Special" prosecutors. Even before the OJ Simpson trial Marcia Clark was a member of the "Special Trials Unit" and these teams attract prosecutors that are looking to make their mark with high profile cases. I'm not saying that they go looking for innocent people to pin charges on but by the time the police have done their part and manufactured a "mountain of evidence" and hand the case over the prosecutors are looking for a win. When the trial of the century falls on your lap you aren't going to objectively question all of the evidence – instead you are going to make excuses for all the pieces that don't fit (EDTA, evidence of multiple assailants, unconstitutional searches, signs of contamination, etc.)

If you are ever called to Jury duty I hope that you won't blindly accept the prosecution's case because "most defendants are guilty". I hope that, regardless of the defendant's social status, you will presume them to be innocent until their guilt has been proven beyond all reasonable doubt before delivering a conviction. Remember too that the prosecution has a ton of dirty tricks up their sleeves.

One particular miscarriage of justice is the fact that **prosecutors can bribe people to testify**. If the defense tells an eyewitness "if you testify for us and help prove our case I will give you 5,000 dollars" that attorney will be disbarred and possibly be incarcerated (as it should be) but the prosecution can go to a convict or co-defendant and get them to turn state's witness in exchange for lighter sentences (sometimes being set free completely). A prosecutor can take 5 years off of a man's sentence just for giving them the testimony they want. Now what is more valuable to you 5,000 dollars or 5 years of your life? Trading testimony for a reduced sentence may be useful to prosecutors but it is an egregious practice that should not be in a so-called free society.

This has been a big chapter so let's just review what we have touched on: we have documented how the **LAPD and the prosecution** in the OJ Simpson trial broke every rule of procedure and common sense in order to squeeze this case into their mold; we dismantled much of the case that was brought against OJ and we even explored the motivations law enforcement and the prosecution have in trying to patch this case against OJ together (these motivations ranged from simply making their job easier to racist world views and career advancement). We have shown how the prosecution **knowingly presented false information** both in the preliminary hearing as well as the criminal trial.

In reality though, we have only scratched the surface when it comes to OJ. For brevity sake we have largely skipped over the ugly civil trial (where the judge approved jurors that were already convinced of his guilt); we didn't touch the disgusting miscarriage of justice known as the "kidnapping" charges levied against OJ in Las Vegas (*that he is still being incarcerated for but we know it was really about the Brentwood murders*), and we **could have dismantled even more of the evidence** (and perhaps we will in a future book devoted exclusively to OJ) like the **extremely tight timeline** (which I've left alone since it is so aptly covered in detail in another volume entitled "Killing Time: *The First Full Investigation into the Unsolved Murders of Nicole Brown Simpson and Ronald Goldman*" by Donald Freed and Raymond Briggs). We could also have dissected the issue surrounding the Bruno Magli shoes that OJ Simpson simply never owned as another example[7]. But regardless of if you are now convinced of OJ's innocence or not it should be evident that in this high profile case the police and the prosecution were on the attack. They weren't just "doing their jobs" but they were out to win this career making case. If nothing else I hope I have awakened you to some of the tricks the state plays in trying their cases and perhaps you will be better prepared in the future **When Prosecutors Attack!**

---

[7] The short version there is that OJ Simpson saved every receipt and dumped them on his accountant and no receipt of buying a pair of Bruno Magli shoes, also police around the country scoured every store in the country these exclusive shoes were sold and no one had sold him a pair, over a year later in the civil trial two photographers send a picture to the same photo processor in the UK (outside of the subpoena jurisdiction of the civil trial) and they magically come back with it appearing that he had the shoes. The fact that the non-blown up pixelated version was in a published magazine before the murders seemed to convince the world that he was wearing the shoes. That irrelevant detail overlooks the fact that the picture published in the sports magazine did not show the soles in recognizable form. Only the doctored blow ups coming back from foreign processing did so.

# OJ SIMPSON: THE WRONG MAN

"Well if OJ didn't do it then who did?" is the mindless question you hear repeated again and again as if there is no reasonable answer to such a question. Thankfully that is not the question that juries are asked to answer. You don't have to prove that someone else committed a crime; you just need to show that there is a reasonable doubt that you were the perpetrator. Given what we know about all of the tricks the state can use to ensure a conviction we should be glad about that high legal standard.

But let's do our best to answer this question anyway. In order to do so we need to first dismantle two misleading statements that were repeated thousands of times in the media, namely that Ron Goldman was "a good Samaritan" and that he was "in the wrong place at the wrong time". These statements seem innocuous but like most sly bits of mainstream propaganda they both have implications that we don't think about when we hear and accept them. Let's squash both at the same time by bluntly stating the inevitable truth that Ron Goldman was a drug dealer, became a confidential informant and he was Nicole's boyfriend (or at least one of her boyfriends). I don't mean any insult to the Goldman family who, regardless of the facts, have lost their beloved family member in such a brutal manner.

Let's dissect. First off if you are unfamiliar with the biblical allegory of "the Good Samaritan" you should already know that this is a huge leap. In the illustration someone overcomes social and ethnic boundaries and goes out of their way for a total stranger that had been beaten; he bandages him up and puts him up at a local inn (effectively on his credit line). In the case of Ron Goldman he was bringing misplaced sunglasses to his girlfriend. Notice how one book[8] describes their relationship:

> *"They exercised and attended dance clubs together, and often met for coffee and meals"*

Ron was noted as playing with her kids and walking the dog with Nicole as well and as neighbor Beverly Newman put it "I thought they were married". Also, Nicole had lit candles, drew a bath, put on music and made sure she was scantily clad in dark negligee when Ron Goldman arrived. In other words they were boyfriend and girlfriend. That isn't a crime but it's important to dismantle the false reality the media has worked hard to establish. Calling him a Good Samaritan suggested that he was just being nice and had no other reason for being there. This was **carefully worded to drive home the lie that Nicole was the target**. See, saying he was "in the wrong place at the wrong time" is a statement that already suggests OJ's guilt (because if Nicole is the target that puts OJ at the top of the suspects list). The reality is much more likely to be that he was followed home to be butchered and that Nicole was in the wrong relationship at the wrong time.

How can I say such a thing? For multiple reasons that all center on motive. One of the biggest hurdles the prosecution just couldn't get over was the fact that OJ Simpson had absolutely no motive for these murders. He was wealthy, dated underwear models, had a surprisingly good relationship with his ex-wife, prior to marrying Nicole they had both signed a prenuptial agreement that left him relatively unscathed by the divorce, he had an incredibly high "Q" rating and was flying around the country on business trips for Hertz and other lucrative ventures. In other words: it was good to be "the Juice" back then. Through the whole trial the prosecution could never put a coherent motive on the

---

[8] "When The Husband Is The Suspect", F. Lee Bailey, Forge.

table. Not to mention that his own children were upstairs and we are to believe he left a pool of blood for them to come down and see? I don't buy it but who would have motive to kill Ron Goldman?

Well, there is one detail about Ron Goldman that the media insisted on overlooking, namely that **Ron Goldman was a confidential informant**. Goldman has a six inch thick police record that has been sealed under California Code Section 6254 (Exemption of Particular Records) which is often referred to as the "snitch" provision and is supposed to protect confidential informants. Now before we go any further shouldn't the fact that you never heard about this before even though the media has devoted years of coverage to this subject? Well, it should especially when you come to realize that this is just the tip of the iceberg and that drug dealing is all over this case.

Now a confidential informant is not the same thing as someone joining the Witness Protection Program and the important difference is between "informing" and "witnessing". People often incorrectly think that "witnessing" refers to seeing something when in fact witnessing is really the testifying, or telling, what you saw (terms like "eye-witness" further confuse things). An informant is just someone that is co-operating with police and providing them with key information and if the police are successful at keeping the informant confidential they often don't need new personalities or relocation. The information alone (without sworn testimony) is often useful enough to police for them to strike deals with the informant and this is especially true when the authorities are trying to infiltrate a drug cartel or other organized crime organization. We will get into Ron's background with drugs and how he might have become an informant in the first place but doesn't that just scream of motive? If you are an informant there has to be someone on whom you are informing. But if these informants are supposed to be "confidential" how can word get back that you have snitched?

Of course, if you were a drug kingpin or mafia family head and had excessive amounts of untraceable cash flow wouldn't you try and get a few cops on your payroll? Just like buying politicians there is a surprising array of quasi-legitimate avenues to do exactly that if a cop isn't completely dirty and won't take outright bribes (lucrative security details for "side money", employing family members, etc.)

However it is done, it does occur (even if most cops are honorable it only takes a few) and news of Ron Goldman's loose lips may have gotten back to the wrong set of ears. Before we get deeper into how drugs play into this case, am I being overly dramatic about sinister drug lords putting out "hits" – have I just seen one too many film adaptations of Tom Clancy novels?

## Narco-Restaurateurs

Well, in order to answer that I need to first introduce you to a term that crystalizes what was going on in this case and that term is "Narco-Restaurateur" and it refers to someone that operates a major drug trade through a restaurant. Now, if you are living in some sleepy town in Indiana, this may sound way over the top but this is a very well-documented phenomenon in major cities (especially LA/Hollywood, Miami, New York, Chicago, etc.) The reason this is often used as a front is that a restaurant provides a lot of benefits to a drug lord. A restaurant takes in a **lot of hard cash** (or at least is expected to when evaluated by the IRS) and can be **used to clean money** by faking cash receipts (in fact most privately owned restaurants employ a simple "cash accounting" method that is very easy to manipulate); a restaurant always has young people to work there that are low income and thus are easily impressed with small chunks of dirty money; a restaurant provides a **perfect place to meet** without anyone asking questions (not to mention a **kitchen exit** to help someone split when needed); a high-end restaurant especially provides a perfect way to schmooze and get to know **high income patrons** that are looking for more than tiramisu after their meal; in a crime family this is an easy way to put lower level family members on the payroll so they can have a **legitimate-looking source of income** and lastly there is always food around.

In the mid 1990's there were several Narco-Restaurateurs in the L.A., Santa Monica and Malibu area. The most obvious is the Mezzaluna which has had more than one of its waiters killed. Obviously Ron Goldman makes one; next up is **Michael Nigg**. Like Ron, Michael was a waiter at Mezzaluna and was also an aspiring actor (no surprise that they were friends) and worked with Ron up until a month before the Bundy murders. Unfortunately, like Ron he was also murdered. In September 1995, Nigg was shot in the head in what authorities deemed a "robbery" even though nothing had been taken. Also, his then girlfriend Julie Long was left unharmed and what is even harder to explain (without involving LA's drug underworld) is how this **simple waiter was able to own a Mercedes Benz** at the time of his death (just months after working at Mezzaluna with Ron). It starts to become clear when you realize that Michael Nigg was actually a transplant from Colorado where there is another Mezzaluna (Narco-Restaurant) which happens to be the only Mezzaluna that hasn't closed down since the Bundy murders (remember media attention and scrutiny is not helpful for a Narco-Restaurant). At the time the Mezzaluna syndicate had three locations: Aspen (CO), Beverly Hills (CA) and of course the Brentwood (CA) location where Nigg and Goldman worked.[9] These three locations were collectively managed by a man named **Keith Douglas Zlomsowitch**, a man that the prosecution would not dare put on the witness stand.

Part of the prosecution's case, as we have discussed, was that OJ was this horrible wife beater. They even used a 911 call from 1993 in which OJ didn't even touch Nicole, let alone beat her. The call though showed that OJ was in the background yelling. What was he yelling about? Well, part of it was her cocaine use while the kids were with her but even more interesting is that he had come by Bundy (where his children lived) and as he approached he saw Nicole having sex with the curtains drawn for any passerby to see. With his kids living in the house he was upset about this and, thus, the yelling from the 911 call. But who was Nicole "getting it on" with when OJ dropped by? Well, it was none other than Keith Zlomsowitch.

This man was surrounded by rumors of drug trafficking out of the Mezzaluna Brentwood location and he was even stopped in a car that was trafficking cocaine but only the driver was charged (she naturally claimed that it belonged to Keith). But you know when I heard that detail I thought it was a little thin by itself… I mean maybe this is just a regular old restaurant manager. Well, if so the prosecution would have put him on the stand to sell the theory that OJ was jealous since he

---

[9] In my research I have seen a few claims that as many as **16 employees** working at Mezzaluna have been **murdered**. I have been unable to confirm all of the names or confirm if this number includes all three locations or if it is specifically in connection with the Mezzaluna in Brentwood.

could attest to how OJ reacted in a scenario that would push the jealousy button like none other.

The truth is that the prosecution decided to skip calling him as a witness when they found out about his connections to the cocaine subculture that Nicole, Faye Resnick, and Goldman had been a part of since the Mezzaluna restaurant in Brentwood was under local and federal investigation for illegal drug trafficking (also they were starting to realize that the jealousy angle was manufactured anyhow). Of course Zlomsowitch also managed the Colorado branch which was also under police surveillance.

This would have been more than enough for OJ's defense team to create an alternate plausible theory (if Judge Ito allowed them to go there). There was another reason to call Zlomsowitch and that is to refute the baseless claim that OJ was jealous over Nicole's new lovers (since he was one). On this point **F. Lee Baily is quoted** by the New York Daily News[10] as stating the following:

> *"The public never heard from Zlomsowitch, even though his testimony would have posed a powerful contradiction to the prosecution's only claim of motive: that Simpson killed Nicole because of a jealous rage. We had him under subpoena and were prepared to call him, but like so much other critical evidence, the* ***threat of further erosion of the jury*** *was just too great."*

See, as the defense team was making headway with the Jury the court began to dismiss jurors that either displayed a strong leaning sympathetic to the defense or had backgrounds that would favor the defense team's version of new evidence they were unearthing. Beyond simple erosion the nuclear option of a mistrial loomed over the defense team as well.

Also, Faye Resnick who was an admitted coke-head had moved in with Nicole that June and now we could establish that **Nicole had slept with the manager of the Narco-Restaurant** where Ron Goldman also worked. The following two charts explore these connections in more detail.

---

[10] "OJ Simpson's ex lawyer, F. Lee Baily, claims he can prove the ex-football player is innocent", Nina Mandell, SUNDAY, JANUARY 9, 2011

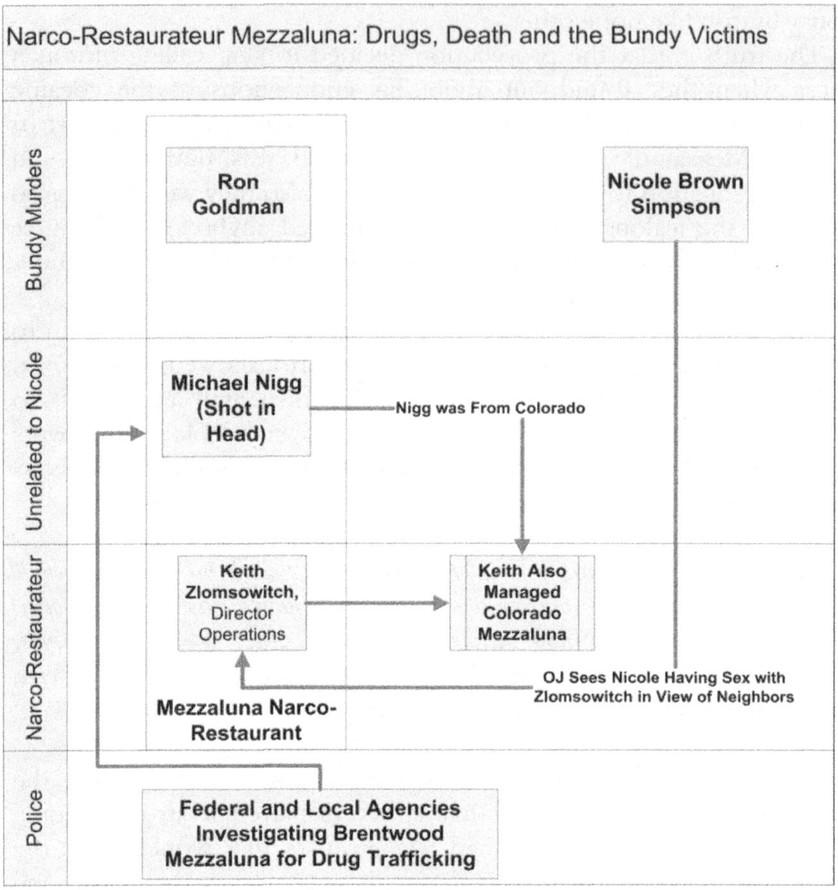


***Figure 11:*** *Ron, Nicole and Michael Nigg Murdered*

Back to murders associated with Ron Goldman, in addition to **Michael Nigg** you have club owner **Brett Cantor** who was not only friends to some degree with Ron Goldman but was also **stabbed to death** in nearly the same fashion that Ron was and his head (about to get graphic here) was almost completely decapitated from the knife murder much like Nicole was on her last night. Those more familiar with decoding autopsy reports than I have said that Brett Cantor's autopsy report was very similar to Ron and Nicole's. Also, he was followed home and **killed in his front yard** essentially just like the Bundy murders. Brett managed a club called **Dragonfly** which was a

Narco-Nightclub that Nicole and Ron regularly frequented (and employees there confirmed they had seen Goldman and Cantor talking more than once so they definitely knew each other).

Getting back to the Mezzaluna several employees have shown up murdered. One of the waiters survived a car bomb as well. See, I bet at your place of business none of your co-workers have ever been targeted with a car bomb; my point is that everyone assumed it was OJ not because of race but because in our more normal lives when a wife or ex-wife is killed it is usually the husband/boyfriend/ex-husband[11]. Check out the next diagram (**Figure** ) for just a sampling of the **Narco-Restaurants in the LA area** (and a few related murders). I don't even mention the Monkey Bar which Zlomsowitch also ran or a half dozen other Narco-Restaurants I could have included. These are just the ones that were easy to tie back to this case in some manner and have solid evidence of being drug fronts.

As the flow chart shows, in one way or another they all have ties back to the Bundy murder victims. In researching this I found it a little difficult to keep track of all of these names that I had never heard nor cared about before so I hope these swim-lane diagrams are helping. To add to what's on the charts, let's discuss **Joey Ippolito** and his Malibu drug front (or Narco-Restaurant) named **Cent'Anni** which by itself was a very fashionable and highly rated Italian restaurant. Joey Ippolito is essentially "second-generation Mafia" and is one of several powerful successors of Meyer Lansky (who was known as the "Mob's Accountant" and made Las Vegas into the international gambling headquarters it is today).

Ippolito even shared the same high security subdivision as Meyer Lansky and wielded a considerable amount of influence within "The Combination"[12] from the northeast to the southwest of the country.

[11] Actually according to researchers from the London School of Hygiene & Tropical Medicine in London who compiled data on nearly 500,000 homicides from 66 countries, only about a third (38.6%) of murdered women was killed by a husband, partner or ex-partner.

[12] The term "The Combination" is often used to refer to the combination of crime families that co-operate within the US; however, many claim this term was originally referring to the *combining* of the **Mafia and the CIA** (examples of this combination at work was the mob-backed assassination attempts on **Fidel**

Now, **Ippolito is inextricably linked with AC Cowling** (who was the driver in the famous "low-speed chase" that was not a chase, dated Denise Brown and was the boyfriend of OJ's first wife prior to them getting married – so he is also tightly joined with the Simpson and Brown families as well).

Cowling was a close associate of Ippolito and was actually staying at his apartment when authorities busted in to arrest Ippolito for supplying drugs to the Santa Monica and Brentwood communities (Ippolito was not there during the bust). Al Cowlings is also said to have been his part-time bodyguard and chauffeur. Cowling and Ippolito also share the same lawyer, namely Donald Re, and Cowlings even testified in front of a grand jury in Ippolito's behalf[13] stating that the Narco-Restaurateur had helped him kick his cocaine habit (so Cowlings is not without a sense of humor).

Did the prosecution call AC Cowling to the witness stand since in their minds he was part of a failed "getaway plan"? No they did not. The prosecution may have kept Cowlings off the stand because bringing him in would have opened the possibility of bringing organized crime into the criminal trial and along with it the scenario that some kind of professional hit man (or men) committed these murders would have presented the Jury with an alternate killer theory.

---

**Castro** and some argue in the murder of **Lee Harvey Oswald** by Jack Ruby).

[13] In fact, this was roughly during the same time as the Simpson Civil Trial so one day he would show up to speak on Ippolito's behalf and the next day show up to the same courthouse to testify on the OJ matter.

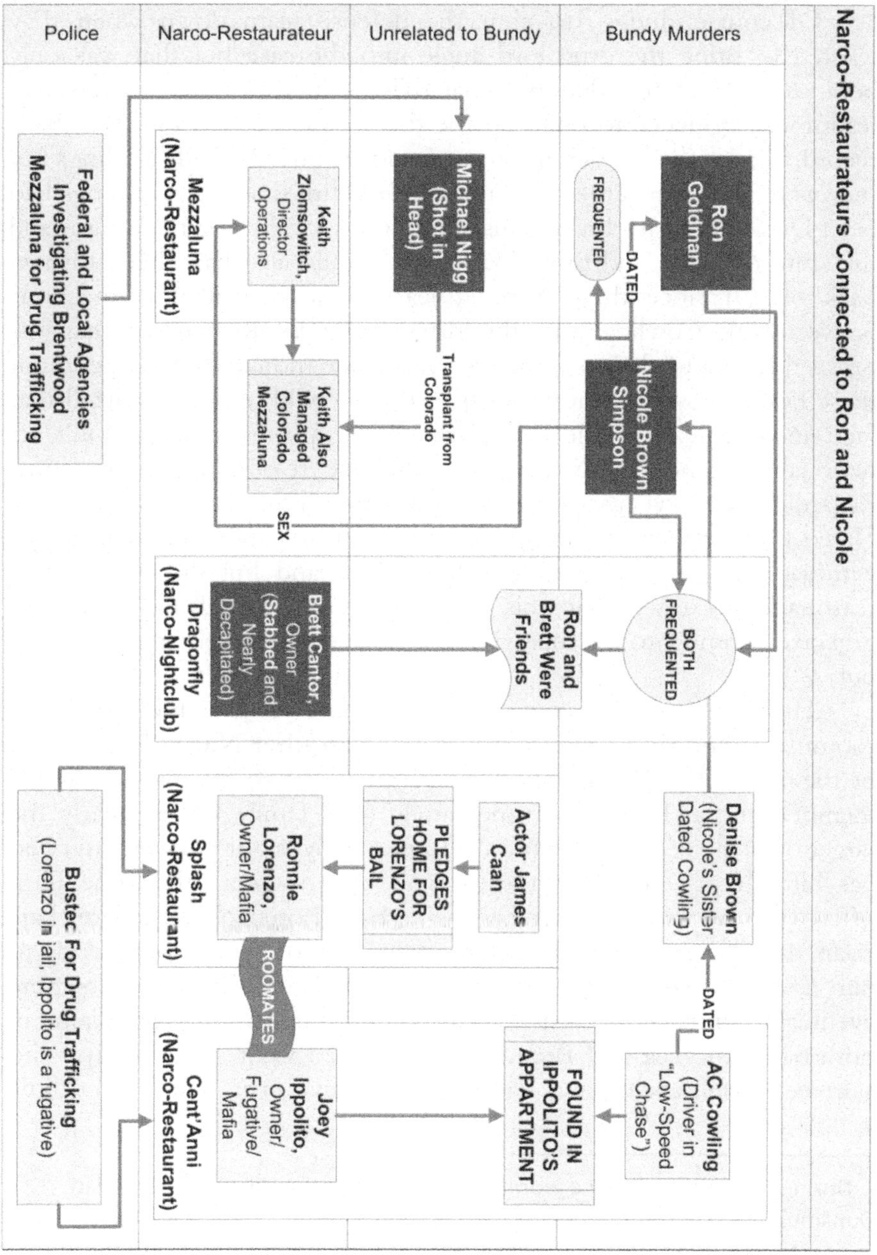


***Figure 12:*** *A Few Drug Fronts Connected to Bundy Murders*

Of course, Judge Ito shut the defense team down when they wanted to bring the drug lord angle into the case but that was only because it lacked foundation. That ruling could have been reversed if testimonial evidence to build up the theory was allowed into the trial's record. To be fair the defense team could also have called Cowlings but they were likely concerned that it could backfire since AC Cowlings had been Denise Brown's lover (thus splitting his loyalty at a minimum) and the smut of drugs and mob connections could also have been thrown back on OJ since there were at least some tangential connections between OJ, Cowling and the drug scene.[14] Remember that the prosecution had failed to show any reasonable motive for OJ to commit these homicides so connecting OJ to drugs could have neutralized that fact since (at least in the Jurors' minds) people on cocaine don't act reasonably or necessarily need a reasonable reason to kill someone. Regardless, we have a solid connection between the Brown sisters and a Narco-Restaurateur. Getting back to the prosecution this makes two witnesses they had reason to call to the stand but didn't and it is reasonable to infer that this is because they could have brought organized crime into the mix which they were desperately trying to keep out.

Then we can slide over on the chart and see that Joey Ippolito's roommate, **Ronnie Lorenzo,** was running **another Narco-Restaurant** by the name of **"Splash"** based in Malibu. Lorenzo was also a fraternal member of the Bonnano crime family (this family was regularly the target of organized crime probes). Interestingly, actor James Caan (who has himself played the part of a mob boss in more than one film) offered his home as collateral to help cover Lorenzo's $2-million bail. Caan also appeared as a character witness for Mr. Lorenzo referring to him as his "best friend". Regardless, both Narco-Restaurateurs were eventually sentenced to ten years hard time for distributing cocaine in both Santa Monica and Brentwood. Lorenzo went away but Ippolito skirted the sentencing and has been a fugitive ever since. One little

[14] During OJ's criminal trial a woman named Samantha Hill was arrested in Dunsmuir (CA) supposedly with over ten pounds of cocaine in her suitcase. Her connections back to AC and OJ were that she was carrying drugs prescribed to Cowlings and in her electronic organizer she had the addresses of both Cowling and Simpson.

wrinkle here is that Joey Ippolito became a fugitive just **three weeks** before Ron and Nicole were brutally murdered in the mob execution style that had previously taken Brett Cantor's life.

So we have established that there are multiple Narco-Restaurants surrounding Ron Goldman and Nicole Simpson (and let's not forget Faye Resnick) including the Mezzaluna where he worked the night of his death. So why would someone from one of these establishments want to kill a low level waiter like Ron Goldman or Nicole for that matter? Well, try and put yourself in the shoes of a Narco-Restaurateur for a moment and ask yourself: what are the top three types of people you would hate? I came up with: **competitors**, **thieves** and above all **snitches**.

## Competition and Thieving

Starting with competition, how might such a lowly waiter come onto a mobster's radar? First, let's review the evidence that Ron Goldman was in fact involved in at least low level drug trading. On that front there has been a great deal of enlightening information that has come out due to the tireless work of the Ocean Medical Investigative Group, one of the only groups that continued its efforts to exonerate OJ Simpson after the trials were over. This group was founded initially by the Johnson bothers, one being an M.D. (an internist actually) and the other being a private investigator/author. Since this case involved so much contention around the autopsy reports and with so many players involved requiring investigative legwork they made a perfect team to start unearthing exonerating documents, leads and analysis.

Eye witnesses called Johnson's investigative group claiming they saw **Ron Goldman selling drugs** near the Cheviot Hills tennis courts in LA[15]. They alleged that he served drug buyers in the parking lot of the tennis courts where he was hired to give tennis lessons as the clubhouse pro.

[15] All references in this chapter to Johnson's investigative group in this chapter are of data collected in their extensive volume "Pursuit of Exhibit 35 in the OJ Simpson murder trial: and its Hidden Secrets", by T.H. Johnson.

An eye witness claimed that her group of concerned residents complained to park officials about Goldman's activities of selling drugs. The alleger claimed that park officials at Cheviot Hills did little to curb the drug activity until, as she claimed, her group took photos of the transactions and turned them over to the officials. The woman claimed that this brought an end to the open drug trafficking and may have resulted in Goldman's termination.

Of course, that is all small potatoes and doesn't get someone professionally "wacked" so to speak. Well, then we know Goldman eventually landed his job as a "waiter" at the Mezzaluna, a restaurant that was under investigation for being a Narco-Restaurant drug front. If nothing else we have already documented that three of its waiters were killed under non-typical circumstances (Columbian necktie, gunshot in a theft-less "mugging", and a car bomb just to name a few). I doubt your local Italian restaurant has racked up so many suspiciously murdered waiters.

While at Mezzaluna, Goldman was able to gain valuable insight into the inner workings of a functioning restaurant (because all of these Narco-Restaurants were also legitimate restaurants in their own right – in fact many received high marks in Zagat and later in online food sites). In addition, he most likely gained valuable contacts in terms of clients and possibly suppliers when it comes to the drug trade. What we don't have to speculate about though is that eventually it occurred to Ron Goldman that he **wanted to open his own Italian "restaurant"** and that is where Nicole Brown Simpson and Faye Resnick come into the picture.

Now in any partnership there are four essential things that need to be brought to the table, namely **expertise, connections, grunt work and of course resources** (read: money) and every partnership divvies up these contributions differently. While Goldman should not have had any issue bringing the first three to the table a waiter (even one that doubles as a small time drug dealer) is going to need a considerable amount of funds to get a restaurant started. Who has large sums of money but not the sense to invest it wisely? You guessed it, the real housewives (and ex-wives) of Los Angeles County. I don't mean to pick on the late Nicole Brown Simpson but it does seem that the Brown sisters were raised to bag wealthy quasi-famous suitors. I mean practically the day Denise turned 18 she was sleeping with Robert Evans

(Paramount studio executive and producer of "The Godfather") and Nicole met and started with OJ when she was 18 soon after her high school graduation. The family business was treating Nicole pretty well who had steady income, a nice place to live, and a half million dollar divorce settlement.

They say birds of a feather flock together and that was certainly the case with Nicole's friend Faye Resnick who was living with Nicole at the time of the murders. Besides being addicted to cocaine, Resnick was working on her fourth marriage at the time. Her third marriage was to Paul Resnick whose wealth stemmed from refurbishing hotels. They divorced in 1991 which netted Faye with a lump sum payout of $194,000 dollars.[16] Of course, a solid cocaine habit can cost thousands a week but perhaps some of this money was still around when her friend Nicole was murdered alongside her boyfriend.

Either way, the three of them had plans to start a restaurant and apparently Ron had already worked out the menu and who knows what other details. Were they killed off by some rival Narco-Restaurateur that didn't want the competition? Well, this trio certainly seems like tiny Minos swimming in a very big and dangerous lake of drug trafficking if they were planning to compete with the likes of Joey Ippolito, Ronnie Lorenzo, or even Keith Zlomsowitch. Certainly that would at least be a motive you could understand (whereas the prosecution struggled to muster up a motive and had to resort to lying to the jury to try and create one – see previous chapter).

The other possibility is one that OJ's defense team tried to run up the flagpole until they were shut down by Judge Ito. Notice the following excerpt that was printed in the Chicago Tribune[17]:

> *Superior Court Judge Lance Ito prohibited Christian Reichardt from testifying about the drug problem of his former girlfriend, Faye Resnick, who stayed with Nicole Simpson for several days before the murders. The defense has suggested*

---

[16] According to New York Magazine, March 20, 1995, Paul Resnick's daughter Jackie stated that Faye "was the absolute worst of his [five] nightmare ex-wives. She put a great strain on our relationship". *Doesn't she sound like a real peach?*

[17] "Testimony on Resnick Drugs Barred", Chicago Tribune. July 13, 1995

> *that Nicole Simpson and friend Ronald Goldman were murdered by drug dealers seeking to send a message to Resnick because she failed to pay for her drugs. But Ito said the defense failed to provide enough direct or circumstantial evidence that the scenario was possible. "I find that* ***the offer of proof regarding motive*** *to be highly speculative," Ito said* (emphasis ours)

I find it sadly comical that Judge Ito dismissed this theory because it didn't offer proof of motive when the prosecution could also not accomplish that in its murder theory that OJ committed these crimes. I mean the idea that OJ, who was sleeping with underwear models and living the "high life" from most people's perspective, killed Nicole in a jealous rage that spilled over onto Ron Goldman is the definition of "highly speculative". That aside, this theory should not be dismissed out of hand because while bookies and other loan sharks tend to not murder their debtors (since "dead men don't pay debts") **people do indeed get murdered for unpaid debts**.

I could name you dozens of homicides where an unpaid debt was the official motive. Recently in Ormond Beach, Florida police arrested Dillon O'Donnell for the murder of **William Davis** over what they say amounted to a small debt. Paul Huebl, the top private investigator of **Whitney Houston's** untimely death claims that she was in fact murdered by drug dealers over unpaid debt. The same goes for **"DJ Megatron"**, 44-year-old **Daniel Finnan** (murdered by Jason Collins who stabbed and set him on fire over an unpaid debt), and countless others that have been killed over unpaid debt. I only bring up these unrelated cases because many people walk around with the incorrect notion that people aren't killed over debts simply because "dead men don't pay debts", an idea that is spread because it sounds sensible. But, that's like saying "foreclosed homeowners don't pay mortgages" yet the fear of foreclosure motivates the rest of us to make our payments faithfully (and these days I don't mind comparing the banks to loan sharks).

Getting back to Resnick, how did she become tied to these murders? Faye Resnick moved in with Nicole Brown Simpson on or about June 3rd of 1994[18]. There are indications, as noted, that she was massively in debt to potentially vicious drug dealers. So what does she

[18] Toobin, Jeffrey. "Blaming Faye?", The New Yorker, February 6, 1995 (Pg. 32)

do? She hides out at a drug treatment facility on June 8th. On June 12th, a person or (more likely) persons brutally murder, at Nicole's residence, both Nicole Simpson and Ron Goldman.

After the brutal murders Resnick is said to be "paranoid". Essentially, she is afraid that she too will be killed.[19] Was the murder an attempt to scare her into paying her drug debt? Did she finance her cocaine habit with money that was given as an investment for their Narco-Restaurateur venture (in other words was there a fourth partner)? We don't know exactly, but Faye was allegedly around $300,000 in debt when she leaves the drug treatment facility and teams up with a Mike Walker of The National Enquirer to write her book. They hide out in Vermont, all the way on the other side of the country. While there, Resnick is still "paranoid" someone might kill her[20]. Now keep in mind that at this point OJ Simpson is in custody so she is not in fear of him hopping out from behind a nearby maple tree with a knit cap and a knife like in some South Park episode.

But if you were afraid that someone was coming after you why would you go and write a book? Shouldn't you be trying to flee the country or change your identity? Well, remember that Faye Resnick was now inextricably linked to the trial of the century and was the "best friend" of the female victim. Publishers were falling over themselves for an anti-OJ book from Resnick and for her it was the easiest way to quickly raise the money needed to pay off her drug debts. That is exactly what happened. When she received her first lump sum it quickly transferred out of her account and then Faye is free again to remain in southern California (lost in my mountain of research I did have a citation for this part so please excuse it's omission).

So far we have established that the Brown/Goldman/Resnick trio was **planning on opening a restaurant** (which if it was anything like the Mezzaluna where Goldman worked would have been another Narco-Restaurant drug front) and the other Narco-Restaurateurs may have not wanted these small players competing with them in their pond and could have easily wiped them out before it got off the ground. That is one very plausible scenario that establishes a coherent motive. Remember, even though they would have been amateurs and been very

---

[19] Toobin, Jeffrey. "Blaming Faye?", The New Yorker, February 6, 1995 (Pg. 34)
[20] Toobin (Pg. 35)

light competition for the more established Narco-Restaurateurs, they may have wanted to simply keep amateurs operating in their arena and drawing unwanted police attention to those types of operations; it's like if you are up to something illegal you don't want to be anywhere near the fumbling loud mouth friend that could blow it for everyone.

Then we have established that **Faye Resnick** had a severe addiction to cocaine (requiring multiple trips to rehab) and we have shown evidence of her having **large dope debt bills** to pay. If this was debt directly generated from unpaid drugs or investment money that she decided to snort up we don't know – either way the money went up her nose and there would be some very unhappy shady character looking for restitution or vengeance. While I consider either of these scenarios to be strong possibilities there is a much simpler answer that can provide a much more direct and clear motive: the killing of a canary.

## Snitches, Informants and Witnesses

There are several confidential informants connected to the Bundy murders but we are only going to focus on two: Ron Goldman and Glen Rogers. Confidential informants come in many shapes and sizes. Usually people act as confidential informants in order to lower or **remove charges against themselves in exchange** for providing law enforcement with key information needed to make a more valuable arrest. This is the type of confidential informant that most people are familiar with however at times confidential informants are paid by law enforcement. In fact, the **FBI regularly retains informants on their payroll** and this shows up occasionally in connection with highly publicized events (although the role of confidential informants is often ignored or kept hidden). For example, it came out years later that Lee Harvey Oswald was on the FBI payroll prior to the **JFK Assassination**, as was Emad Salem in connection with the **1993 World Trade Center Bombing** *(while there is debate over what this meant for the former, the latter was proven to be connected to the event because he recorded his conversations with his FBI handlers including the conversation where they discuss replacing the fake bomb with a real explosive device).*

Getting back to this case, in September of 2000, T.H. Johnson[21] went to a courthouse in Malibu to review a criminal traffic case of Ronald Lyle Goldman. After the clerk typed in the file number (**91C00362**) into the computer, it started to print out approximately three feet of paper with court information. This single criminal traffic case showed major traffic violations. Given Goldman's continued suspended license status and over $16,000 in bench warrants, these offenses would normally carry jail time. I sent my own investigator to Malibu (actually it was my editor who happened to be in the Santa Monica/Malibu area) and they have since permanently closed down the courthouse there and their files were apparently sent to Van Nuys where we are still pursuing this case file (but don't really expect to get any further than the Ocean Medical Investigative Group got). Goldman continued to receive lenient treatment from several judges, get released, borrow a car and continue the same behavior.

Why such repeated leniency from the courts? Why wasn't Goldman more concerned with the consequences of his brazen attitude? Well, certainly if you have a "get out of jail free card" that might affect your behavior, don't you think? Goldman was a confidential informant so as long as he didn't screw up too hugely he could rely on his government handler to cover his back for the little stuff. How can we say that? Well, for many reasons but we will focus just on the fact that Goldman's criminal record **inexplicitly vanishes** at every turn and the more important fact that **Section 6254** (known as the "snitch" provision) is **repeatedly cited** for denying requests to see Goldman's files (the ones that haven't mysteriously been destroyed).

See, later when Johnson discovered a $10,000 warrant for a probation violation he asked to see the rest of the file. A superior at the courthouse stated that it had been **destroyed five years earlier** in 1995. But Goldman's file wouldn't be eligible for destruction until 2001 (ten years after the 1991 case) but in deviation of standard procedures it was destroyed and cannot be obtained.

They even searched the DMV using Goldman's name, DOB and SS number and as of 11/9/00 they had **nothing on file** (it's like he never existed).

---

[21] Investigative Team Leader, Ocean Medical Investigative Group and author of "Pursuit of Exhibit 35 in the OJ Simpson murder trial: and its Hidden Secrets".

Johnson goes back to the Malibu courthouse, where a different clerk finds the file. It is six inches thick so it doesn't fit thru the grating separating Johnson from the clerk. In the time it took to step over to the service window (which had a larger opening), a female superior stopped the clerk from handing over the file.

On December 15, 2000, T.H. Johnson sent certified letters to the four judges associated with the Goldman file, including Judge **Robert Ma**, Judge **Reva Goet** and Judge **Susan G. Carl** (they don't state the fourth Judge's name for some reason), describing the incident.

In January 2001 he returns to the Malibu courthouse, after receiving **no response from any of the justices**. At first he is told by a clerk that the basement flooded due to heavy winter rains, and **Goldman's file had been destroyed in the rain**! So far we are up to mysterious records destruction, documents sealed because he was a confidential informant and now a so-called "act of God" keeping Goldman's true background from coming out.

Johnson then speaks to the office manager, Ann Maden, Manager of the Malibu Municipal Court Clerk's Office. She received the certified letters and interviewed her staff about the incident. Staff claimed they tried to offer him the file, but he just up and left for no reason. He then asks if he can see the file (now in her hands). What was her response? "I can't let you do that. This file is **protected by Section 6254**, Attachment B."

Section 6254, attachment B is part of the law code in California restricting criminal history records from normal public access. A later request prompted a letter from the Risk Management Division of the LA Police Department denying a public access request of one of the Goldman records pursuant to Section 6254 (F). I am still in search of more corroborating evidence, but it appears that **Faye Resnick** herself has criminal records that are also **protected by this so-called "snitch provision"** (Section 6254). So in this Narco-Restaurant trio we have at least two snitches! I mean it could be that their deaths were not directly connected to their co-operation with law enforcement but shouldn't we be outraged that the mainstream media covered this case non-stop for **over a year and we were never told** this important piece of information?

So, this appears to be the clearest cut motive for murder. You've all seen this played out in mafia-themed films: low level operative is caught, sings "like a canary" and snitches on higher ups to reduce their charges or sentence, and of course the higher ups have them killed. But does this fit the facts of this particular case?

The short answer is absolutely yes. This had all the appearances of a drug hit carried out by multiple assailants. We have the eye witnesses to back this up. Before getting into that remember that the prosecution tried to make it out that the stab wounds showed "personal rage" but in reality there is no calm and collected business-like way to stab someone to death. Getting stabbed by a jilted lover or a ruthless drug trafficking assailant cannot be forensically distinguished (and remember the pathologist the prosecution put on the stand was not the coroner that performed the autopsy – they shopped around until they got far enough up the hierarchy to find someone that would sing from their song sheet). We could debate about the wounds but instead we will stick with the eye witnesses. Let's see what they each had to say about how many assailants were present and what their ethnic makeup was. Unfortunately some of these eye witnesses were kept from testifying (a common tactic **When Prosecutors Attack**).

First, we have **Mary Anne Gerchas** who reported seeing four men fleeing the Bundy crime scene. Was this OJ with three of his buddies? Not likely since she reported seeing two Caucasian and two Latin men (no African-American or other blacks present). In his opening statement Johnnie Cochran said that she would testify to the above, so why didn't she testify? After being announced as a witness Ms. Gerchas was subjected to an unfathomable string of prosecutorial attacks from the state on the most baseless grounds. They went after her for "irregularities" in her car loan application! Not her tax return, not in her testimony but on a car loan! The next offense had to do with an unpaid hotel bill if you can believe it. Her attorney William Graysen called it a **"campaign of intimidation"** and had this to say on the lack of wisdom of such an attack:

> *"It can only hurt prosecutors, because it shows* ***they are attempting to hide the truth.*** *That gives her credibility"* (emphasis ours).

Next up we have **Frank Chiuchiolo** who wasn't called by the defense team because he was a convict. That said, while he happened to be casing a house for a burglary, Chiuchiolo said he saw Caucasian and Latino men at the crime scene about the time of the murder as well. Not the most reliable witness on his own but the fact that his testimony independently corroborates other testimony suggests it was not fabricated (what are the chances of multiple witnesses fabricating their testimony with harmonious details?)

One witness that you just have to trust is **Leif Tilden** if for no other reason that he was the actor that played Donatello in the first two Teenage Mutant Ninja Turtles movies (I know this is a serious subject but a little humor is needed to keep your sanity). Mr. Tilden told the prosecution that **he saw four** non-African American's at the crime scene about the time of the murders (between 10 and 10:30). Some reports say that he said they were Caucasian but he actually just stated that he could tell **they were not black** so this fits perfectly with the other testimony that two Latinos and two non-Latin whites where at the crime scene. Without the Jury present, Cochran complained to Judge Ito that the prosecution had interviewed Tilden and had not lived up to their responsibility to share discovery (*of course Darden scrambled to clean it up claiming that the interview took place just 24 hours beforehand – this seems like a very tight timeline for word to get back to the defense team*).

Then we come to **Thomas Lang** (not the LAPD Detective Tom Lange but the eye witness Thomas Lang[22]) who lived about two blocks south of Nicole's condo at 875 S. Bundy Drive in Brentwood. Thomas was taking his dog for a walk after returning from a trip out of town (his wife confirmed that he started the walk right after 10 PM). When he approached the block of the crime scene he noticed two important things. First, he saw a white truck which he identified as a Ford F-350 which looks nothing like OJ's Bronco, especially to a man that has **owned not less than eleven Ford trucks** in his life. Several witnesses said they saw some white vehicle but none had Lang's confidence or ability in identifying the exact model. Secondly, and more importantly, Lang saw a blonde woman wearing black clothing (like Nicole was found in) talking with a man standing beside the truck in the street, partially obscured by the F-350's open door and he said she had an angry look on her face. In what Lang described as a "menacing

[22] For clarity the LAPD Detective Tom Lange will not be referenced at all for the rest of this chapter.

posture" was a second man standing behind the blond woman (later identified as Nicole) near the entrance to Nicole's property. His dog was not leashed and he didn't want to get in the middle of their interchange so he turned in the opposite direction before spotting the two additional members of this crew that were likely present. The point though is that neither of these men could have been OJ because he described them as "not black". Beyond that Lang happened to work for a hotel owner that also happened to be a lawyer. This employer/lawyer heard these details from Lang and on June 17th had him record all of his recollections on a tape recorder to create what lawyers call an "establishing point" so that his future testimony couldn't be labeled as being the result of a faded or corrupted memory (in addition he had created a simpler establishing point himself on June 14th, the day after the murders, and even made a sketch of the woman who was obviously Nicole and the two males he had witnessed speaking with her moments before her murder and sent a copy to police who had already charged Simpson at this point).

Tom offered to retrace his steps of the night of June 12th for Officer David Payne of the Robbery-Homicide division of the LAPD but Payne declined the invitation. It should be obvious by now that once a suspect is charged that the police and prosecution are not interested in contradictory leads. That said it is a fair question to ask why Lang never testified. Interestingly, F. Lee Bailey says that throughout the entire trial this is the only time he disagreed with Cochran about whether or not to call a witness but as the defense team lead the decision was Cochran's to make and he didn't make it lightly. Cochran was concerned that, while Mr. **Lang was convinced the car he saw was a Ford F-350**, the prosecution might twist this as confirmation that a white Bronco was at the crime scene since both trucks were Ford's and the jurors were likely not as familiar with these trucks to trust an eye witness making this distinction. Also, the prosecution was really **gunning for a mistrial** since they felt they didn't have the goods[23] and retrials always favor the State since it always has resources whereas individuals are usually sapped from the first trial and

[23] If you doubt this watch the closing arguments which are available online and you will see that the defense team is closing with confidence whereas the prosecution – especially Marcia Clark – seemed very unsure of itself.

are thus disadvantaged the second time around.

Obviously, the defense team didn't need any of these people to testify because they had already obliterated nearly all of the prosecution's case and they did secure a Not Guilty verdict. That said, this brief overview of witnesses seeing multiple whites at the crime scene should at least partially answer the "if not OJ then who" crowd a bit. It is important to remember that **NOT A SINGLE PERSON** testified to having seen OJ Simpson at Bundy that night. Also it was important to look into these witnesses to expose how **When Prosecutors Attack** they use any trick they can to intimidate witnesses from providing exculpatory testimony; they neglect their discovery sharing duty, they are quick to discredit witnesses with unrelated criminal backgrounds (even though they regularly call witnesses they have bribed into testifying) and they will even resort to trumping up charges against defense witnesses as they was the case with Mary Anne Gerchas.

Plus, these are just the named witnesses that can easily be provided at this point. The police received multiple phone leads that were never pursued including a call where an unnamed witness **saw men taking boxes or cartons out of Nicole's condo** around the time of the murders. If Ron, Nicole and Faye were trading in cocaine to raise money for their Narco-Restaurant then they would likely have a sufficient amount on hand and this could very well be what was being hauled out of her home and is a very simple motive for the murders. Whether or not their drug cache was taken in partial payment of Resnick's drug debt cannot be established. We do know that she was paranoid for her own safety until she received her first lump sum payment for her book so we can at least say that her debts were not completely covered until then.

Keep in mind that I have devoted much of this book to the OJ Simpson case which ended in the mid-1990s and my goal has been to expose the tactics and modus operandi of the state **When Prosecutors Attack** so we can examine where we are not learning the lessons we need to and that proving that someone else killed Nicole and Ron has really been a means to that end. That said I would love to tell you explicitly who the real killers are by name but that is not something that can be established beyond all reasonable doubt. That said we have established multiple connections between the murdered and the drug trafficking scene in Southern California. That said is there at least one killer close to Nicole that we can identify by name? In fact there is!

## Narcotics Informant: Glen Rogers

Most of the time, Glen Rogers is introduced as a "serial killer" a term that certainly fits to some degree since he has killed a string of people without any clear motive or provocation (his sister Sue is on record as saying that at one time he claimed to have committed 70 murders – whereas authorities have only nailed him down to 5 murders officially).

***Figure 13:*** *Glen Rogers*

That said, most people have never met a serial killer and thus can only think back to a fictional Hollywood depiction or some dramatic portrayal on *"Unsolved Mysteries"* or something to that effect. Every movie on the subject makes it out that serial killers just come out of nowhere and they are usually well spoken, educated (but not working), white men that are either quoting obscure poetry or blasting classical music while they revel in the retelling of their murderous exploits. The reality doesn't usually match up.

Instead there is usually a slow build up to their spree of killings involving a wide range of other criminal activity. Often they aren't completely random targets but connect in some way to the other parts of their criminal life so that the line between a "drug hit" and a "serial killing" will start to blur. Remember even serial killers need to go through the normal functions of life: eating, sleeping, paying bills, filling up with gas, etc. So, a lot of them are attracted to violent forms of employment like becoming an enforcer for a drug cartel and (for the daring) they can supplement their income by doubling as a narcotics informant and get on the government payroll. Yes, there are thousands of criminals out there that are on the government dole as informants and get lenient treatment when they are picked up for even unrelated offenses. This was the case with Ron Goldman as we've discussed previously and it was certainly the case with Glen Rogers. *This will get a little complicated which is why the next two figures are provided to give you a visual aid to all of these connections.*

First let's dig a little into Glen's background in case you haven't heard of him. Rogers is known today as the "Cross Country Killer" because he has killed in at least 5 states spread across the United States. He grew up in Hamilton, Ohio, with his six siblings and his abusive parents (trust me I am NOT making excuses for this creep) and his mother even tried to beat him out of being left-handed which we will get into more in a bit. As juveniles Glen and his brother Clay would commit all sorts of crimes, although most of them were non-violent in nature (mostly home robberies and petty thefts).

According to Clay Rogers, when they would get picked up by the police they would get treated better than at home (better food, no beatings, etc.) so there was really **no incentive to stay out of trouble**. This lack of effective negative reinforcement would translate to their adult lives as well, at least in the case of Glen Rogers.

See, at some point Glen had been picked up in a massive narcotics sweep that resulted in about 21 people being indicted and not without his help. Glen quietly rolled on the others involved and then started a **10 year stint of working as a paid narcotics** informant with Hamilton, Ohio Narcotics Task Force. In fact, Hamilton, Ohio Police Sgt. Tom Kilgore testified that Rogers had worked for the department as a paid undercover narcotics informant, **making hundreds of cases** over the years **without ever breaking his cover**. But, Glen didn't stop with working just with the Hamilton Police Department. In the documentary "My Brother the Serial Killer" Tom Kilgore is taped saying the following:

> *"Glen is the one that approached the Narcotics unit wanting to be able to work undercover. Glen* ***worked with a lot of different agencies****, and I think those law enforcement agencies may have* ***provided some little training there that helped him kind of get out of some of the problems*** *he was in that maybe had he not seen all that he would have not known how to do it".*

So we learn a few things from Sgt. Kilgore's revealing comments. First we learn that Rogers worked with a wide array of government agencies (and this will come into play a little later). Secondly, besides getting paid and receiving lenient treatment when arrested these informants receive training from our government on how to evade capture from other agencies and work the system to keep them out of trouble. Remember the dirty tricks that are used **When Prosecutors Attack**: bought testimony, trumped up charges, and now employing criminals as agents of law enforcement and training them how to commit crime with impunity? Perhaps it's time to rethink this system.

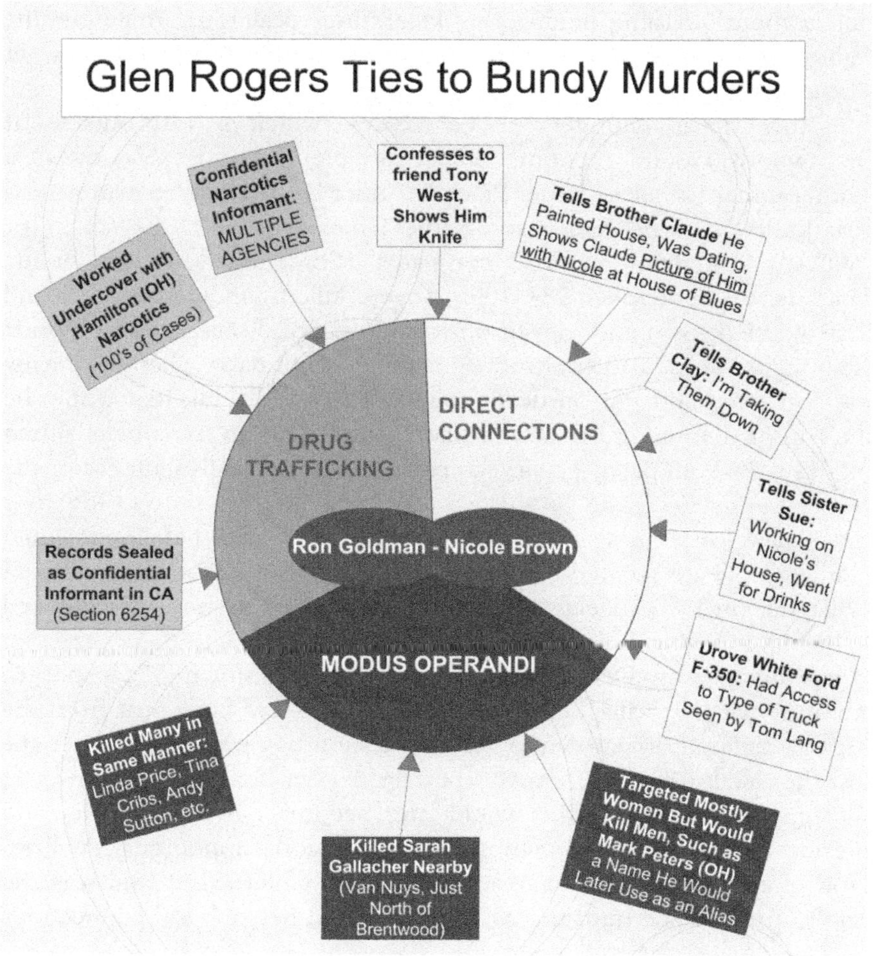


***Figure 14:** Narcotics Informant Tied to Bundy Murders*

I would be very interested to find out specifically to which "agencies" officer Kilgore is referring but the term is usually used for federal bodies and since Glen was an experienced narcotics informant it is reasonable to extrapolate that he was probably in the employ of the FBI and the DEA[24]. Either way, helping to close over 100 narcotics cases in Ohio alone puts him firmly in the middle of the drug trade. Remember, a narcotics informant is essentially just someone that works for the government and works for a drug cartel (a double agent of sorts) but is there anything linking this killer/drug dealer/informant to the California law enforcement community? Well, that is where things get interesting.

Rogers was definitely in Van Nuys (which is just outside of Brentwood) around the time of the double homicide working as a painter under the alias "James Peters" (earlier he had killed a man named "Mark Peters" who had a son name James whose ID he stole) for "William J. Galvin Painting" company. Sometime after the Bundy murders, on September 28th 1995 Rogers killed Sandra Gallagher and then skipped town and moved on to Mississippi, Louisiana and Florida (stabbing a woman to death in each state). Florida is where he finally got convicted and put on death row. You would think that would be the end of the matter but as you may be aware not every convict sitting on death row ultimately gets executed; at times the death sentence or the conviction itself can be overturned on appeal and the state's Governor can always order a stay of execution. To be sure that Glen would ultimately get executed the surviving family members of Sandra Gallagher (in Los Angeles, CA) wanted to make sure he was sentenced to death in California as well as Florida.

Enter Deputy District Attorney (DDA) Lea Purwin D'Agostino to advocate for the Gallagher family. D'Agostino had been sent from the Major Case unit downtown to the sleepy suburbs of Van Nuys after she lost the election for District Attorney against her boss Ira K. Reiner. At the time Gil Garcetti (who would later become District Attorney and preside over the OJ Simpson prosecution appointing William Hodgeman as lead prosecutor) was Reiner's Chief DDA and was the one to process the transfer. D'Agostino used her political connections

---

[24] In the event that our FOIA requests ever get fulfilled we will include those details in a future edition of this volume.

with Governor Pete Wilson to get Glen Rogers transferred from Florida to California to stand trial for what should be an open and shut case. However, extradition requests are usually not honored for convicts sitting on death row (because logically what is the point if they ultimately get executed in the state they are in). These types of extraditions require a Governors agreement which is exactly what it sounds like: two governors from two different states agreeing on the exchange. D'Agostino was not only leaning on her connection with California Governor Pete Wilson but was in regular correspondence with then Florida Governor Lawton Chiles so she was pushing on both sides to come to an agreement. As you can imagine this is no small feat to pull off but the DDA was successful and Rogers was taken off of death row in Florida to stand trial for the Van Nuys murder that of course fell under D'Agostino's jurisdiction. This would have been the highest profile case since she was given the suburban reassignment but the case wouldn't stay with her (*again a lot of these connections may be hard to follow which is why the two diagrams are included to help visually*).

District Attorney Gil Garcetti (who was previously the Chief DDA that with the previous DA had sent D'Agostino packing to Van Nuys) has all of her files confiscated and given to Deputy DA Pat Dixon and gets Superior Court Judge John H. Reid to seal the death row files on Glen Rogers (Judge Reid is also the one that issued the ex-parte order for all the OJ Simpson Criminal files to be removed after the case – an order carried out by Deputy DA Bill Hodgeman).

D'Agostino then files a Civil Service Grievance because of this unwarranted action. These grievances are usually public documents but Judge Reid takes the unusual step of sealing her grievance which mentions Glen Rogers' death row files. What was the government hiding with all of these files that were being sealed and destroyed? Well, interestingly Glen Rogers' file was sealed under the same California statute that protected Ron Goldman's criminal record, namely Section 6254 that protects confidential informants (the snitch provision). Was the government embarrassed that they had employed a man that turned out to be a serial killer? Why at every turn does the state shut down or obfuscate any drug connection to the Simpson case? It should be obvious that, at a minimum, the state doesn't want anyone looking too closely at its hordes of paid criminals it employs to infiltrate drug cartels. In a future volume we will explore this more aspect more deeply but for now let's stick with the case at hand. What direct connections does Rogers have with the OJ Simpson case?

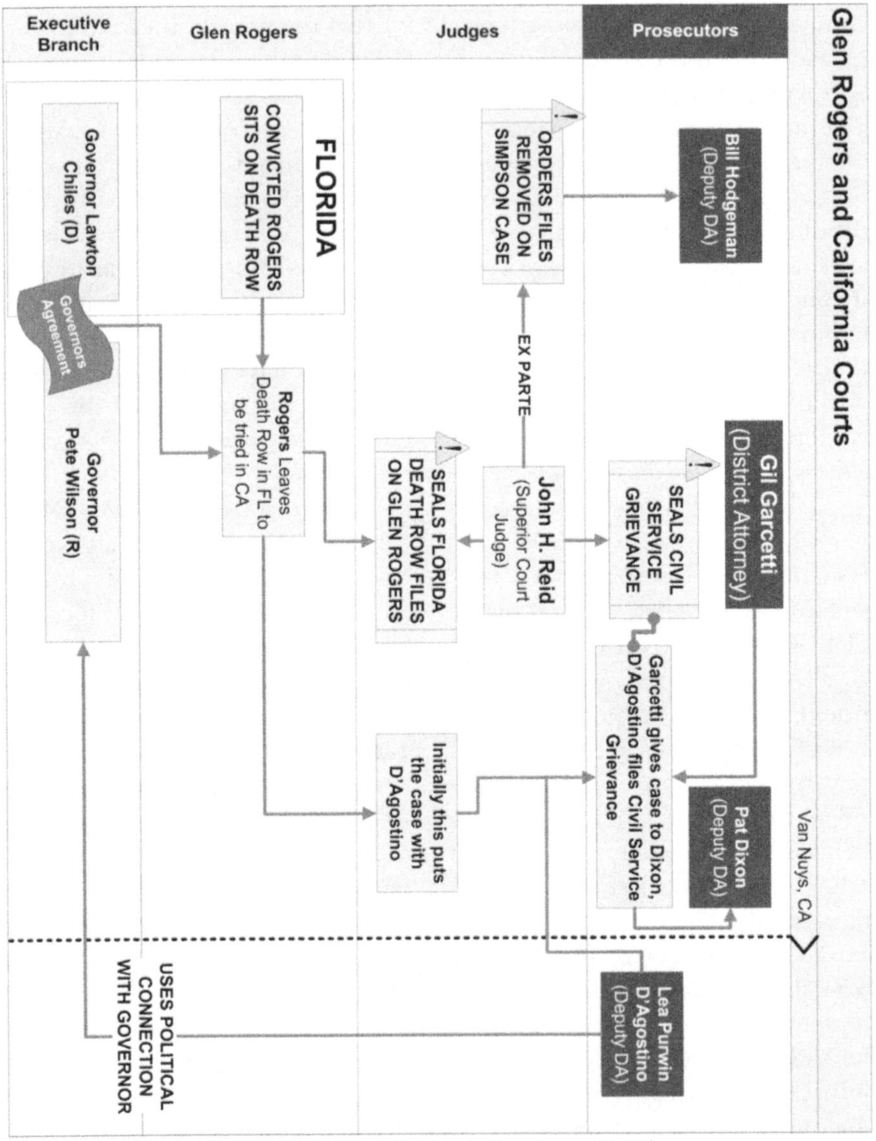


***Figure 15:** Rogers, California Courts and OJ Files*

So far we have covered Glen's extensive connections to drug

trafficking, we have established that he operated in the area around the times of the murder and we have shown that the Bundy murders certainly fit within his Motus Operandi (MO). Now we get to his direct connections which revolve mostly around his comments to family members, friends and in letters with other convicts. This isn't necessarily the most trustworthy group of people but this is what they had to say:

- Glen told his brother Claude he was **dating Nicole**, that he painted her house and even showed him a picture of the two of them together at the "House of Blues"[25]. We know Nicole was dating Ron Goldman but remember that her vanity plate was "L84AD8" as in "late for a date" suggesting she would bounce from date to date presumably with a variety of men.
- Glen tells his sister Sue Rogers that he met a beautiful girl named Nicole that was married to "some black football player" and that he was working on her house. He also claimed that they went for drinks and **Sue is hearing this before the murders** (many have tried to brand Glen Rogers as just a crazy trying to take credit for the murders to gain some twisted fame but if we believe Sue's account that blows away that narrative).
- Glen tells his brother Clay Rogers that **"they got money, they're well off, and I'm taking them down"** in reference to Nicole (who is financially connected to OJ). This may seem like a startling thing to reveal to a sibling but Glen was closest with his brother Clay who had committed numerous crimes together before Glen escalated to killings.
- In the documentary "My Brother the Serial Killer" this same brother (Clay) admits that **"I'm absolutely certain my brother killed Nicole Simpson and Ron Goldman**" (emphasis ours).
- According to Roger's friend Tony West **he confessed to killing Nicole and Ron**. West claims that Glen bragged "I killed them and made it look like OJ did it to frame the

[25] While this photo has never surfaced there was a passing mention of Mark Fuhrman being in possession of a copy of this same photo on Court TV.

n***er". This statement may have been sold to a tabloid so you can decide for yourself but it does seem to be consistent with his family's comments.

- As a painter with "William J. Galvin Painting" company Rogers had access to a white Ford F-350 the model identified by witness Tom Lang *(a man who had owned 11 Ford trucks and knew the difference between a Bronco and an F-350).*
- Deputy DA Lea Purwin D'Agostino got a hold of letters to a fellow convict wherein Roger's cryptically says "**I did [know] Nicole Simpson** and that's all I can say **if you know what I mean**" (read: wink, wink). D'Agostino then forwarded this and other letters from Glen Rogers to the Simpson prosecutors who of course were not interested in anyone but their star defendant.

Not to mention the fact that Glen Rogers is left-handed and favored his left hand in most of his stabbings. The initial autopsy reports suggested that one of the two killers was likely left-handed since many of the fatal wounds were made on the left side of the victims and the prevailing theory is that the killer(s) would be striking from behind.

Now again I don't take the family members to be completely trustworthy. In the documentary clay includes an uncorroborated detail that didn't sit well with me, namely that Rogers claimed that OJ had hired him to retrieve some earrings from Nicole. I felt this was a ridiculous claim since OJ was a multi-millionaire and this detail was not included in any of the other statements made by Glen's family or friends. One of the contributors to the documentary "My Brother the Serial Killer" was **private investigator Pat McKenna** whom I have always respected so I figured I would follow up with him on this point. **In my direct interview with Mr. McKenna** this is what he had to say:

> *"I've always thought that the Glen Rogers* ***story was B.S. at least the part of him being hired by OJ****. Also the scenario where he participated in the killings with OJ is B.S. because in the most honest layout of the timeline* ***OJ had a 6 minute window*** *to commit the murders, dispose of the cloths and murder weapon and get back to Bundy. OJ was simply not involved in these murders and hey there are over 2000 unsolved murders every year and this is just one of them."*

Since I had him on the phone I also asked him about a phrase repeated again and again in the mainstream media, namely "what motive would detectives and prosecutors have in fabricating evidence to make a case against OJ?" This is what he had to say:

> *"Look, these detectives and prosecutors walk around in suits they bought at JCPenny and are looking for every opportunity to hit it big. Of course they have motive to fudge the details to make a high profile case, Marcia Clark and Mark Fuhrman walked away with millions".*

Pat McKenna was the lead private investigator for the Simpson team and in the documentary on Rogers sums up the sentiment of the team investigating on OJ's behalf:

> *"We felt throughout the criminal case, and to this day, that that killer came from the world of Faye Resnick".*

In other words, the killers came from the world of illicit drug trafficking, a world that Glen Rogers was deeply rooted. Rogers knew the drug trade extensively and as we mentioned managed to make over 100 cases in Ohio with their Narcotics Task Force. Likely he was much better at keeping his cover than Ron Goldman was if in fact his snitching was the motive behind his murder. If you are unfamiliar with this underworld it may seem strange that Rogers who is a confidential informant in California (with records sealed under Section 6254) would kill another confidential informant, namely Ron Goldman. But try and wrap your mind around the fact that every narcotics informant works not only for the government but for a narcotics dealer or drug lord. The state gives informants great leeway to operate without blowing their cover in order to take down their allusive "big fish"[26].

---

[26] Some have made the claim that government infiltration into drug cartels has more to do with wanting to take control of these cartels than to actually take them down. While this is way outside of the purview of this book to cover we will just comment that those in this camp cite the CIA drug running which was the lesser known component of the "Iran-Contra" scandal of the 1980's. This would also cast a very different light on the recent "Fast and Furious" scandal where Mexican drug cartels were being armed by the U.S. Justice Department.

After the fact, would officials rather embarrass themselves by implicating one of their confidential operatives[27] or would they prefer to be involved in the case of the century and prosecute a famous athlete and actor? Well, any look at congress should give you the answer. We are years into the Great Recession and there have been no major indictments of banks and Wall Street whereas athletes are brought regularly before congress to testify about the national dilemma of steroid use within professional sports (WHO CARES)! I realize that is a completely unrelated tangent but you get my point.

## CONCLUSIONS

We have spent most of this volume on the OJ Simpson case because it is really a prime example of **When Prosecutors Attack** and it is important not to let this fade into the annals of history without learning the lessons this case had to teach us. I hope it is clear at this point that prosecutors on high profile cases are not interested in conflicting evidence, that they are not interested in unearthing the truth, and are not interested in necessarily finding the right man at the sacrifice of their own careers. We have established lead after lead that was simply not followed up on by the police and prosecution. We have shown how the media can be used to manipulate the public's perception of reality and leave them with convictions devoid of facts.

Unlike the LAPD however you will see that the police in the Roderick Scott and George Zimmerman cases seemed to have acted honorably but both these cases were pushed by prosecutors that did not have any evidence that a crime had even been committed, let alone that the defendants were culpable. We now leave the dark and sleazy underworld of Los Angeles County and enter the otherwise sleepy suburban town of Greece in upstate New York.

---

[27] Remember at this point the Rampart scandal had not come out so right there you have over 70 cases of corruption and planted evidence connected to the CRASH "anti-gang" unit. This is the very same type of operations that would have pulled in the likes of a Glen Rogers as a confidential informant. Again, a future edition will be released if we are successful with our FOIA requests on the subject.

# UNIT TWO: RODERICK SCOTT

# **RODERICK SCOTT**: THE BLACK ZIMMERMAN?

Roderick Scott is a name that you would have never heard of if George Zimmerman had never encountered Trayvon Martin. Still, he is barely mentioned in the media and when he is it is either "look at this case that is exactly like the Zimmerman case" or "look at how racists are trying to compare this old self-defense case involved Mr. Scott with the Zimmerman case". If you've been watching the coverage of the Zimmerman case you have witnessed the two opposed camps locking into position with little interest in giving anything an honest examination. Unlike the network news pundits that need to cram everything into 30 second sound bites we can take the time here to logically hash out these details. It may be a little much to call Roderick Scott the "Black Zimmerman" but these cases are materially pretty similar from a legal perspective and from the prospective of prosecutors being on the attack. They are not *exactly* the same but then no two cases are. **Oprah recently decided to profane the memory of Emmett Till** by comparing him to Trayvon Martin (who, as you will see in the next section, was a violent drug dealer). This could not have been a worse comparison since Emmett Till was a completely innocent victim of racially motivated violence, but we will get into that more in the next section on Zimmerman. For now suffice it to say that the Roderick Scott case is a fair point of comparison for the Zimmerman case and in this section we will hash out the similarities and differences.

If this is the first you are hearing of Roderick Scott he is the middle gentlemen on the cover of this book. He is a black gun owner, husband and I believe home owner that on April 4th (2009) woke up in the middle of the night (around 3 AM) at the sound of some white drug users talking in on his driveway[28].

Scott happened to be downstairs so was the first in his house to hear the voices outside his home on 58 Banberry Way in the Town of Greece, New York. His significant other, Tracy Allen, was upstairs so Roderick went up and told her to call 911. As Tracy is calling 911 she is looking out the window and sees the gang of three heading towards her neighbor's house.

Scott takes his .40 caliber automatic Smith and Wesson sidearm (for which he possessed a Pistol Permit and was properly registered according to New York's Soviet style registration program) with him to investigate but keeps his gun holstered. Scott armed himself for the following reasons:

1. According to the "Factual Background" motion submitted by the defense, when Scott left his home "he had absolutely no idea whether these individuals were armed in any way so he took his permitted handgun".
2. In addition, Scott's stated intention for leaving his house with his handgun was to hold the individuals at bay while the police responded.
3. Lastly, arming oneself is a constitutionally guaranteed right and no one should really ever have to explain why they have armed themselves in this country. The only question should be if there was a legal basis for discharging said firearm at the target in question.

Simply owning or bearing a firearm is starting to become viewed as a crime in itself. After a recent shooting the brain dead media said that police went to the shooter's house and found a "scary arsenal of weapons" as if the man's inventory should be viewed as an existential

[28] The autopsy of Christopher Cervini later showed that he still had at least marijuana still in his system.

threat *(I mean a lone gunman only has two hands so it really doesn't matter how many guns they have at home does it?).*

***Figure 16***: *Self-Defense Shooter Roderick Scott (Left) and Thief Christopher Cervini*

Outside he sees a small gang of white teenagers out in the middle of the night and they are messing with the cars on the street; to Scott it is obvious that they are trying to break in to the cars on his block. By the time Scott reached the three individuals, one of them (namely Brian Hopkins) was standing at the end of the driveway of 39 Banberry Way and to Scott it appeared he was acting as "a lookout". The other two (James Cervini and the late Christopher Cervini) were closer to the house in between two vehicles. As Scott approached the "lookout", Hopkins, left running (later he would be the most forthcoming of the two surviving teens in testifying to their criminal behavior that night).

If you are not familiar with upstate New York than you might not realize that the first week of April can be very cold and on this night the temperature was about 35 degrees Fahrenheit with the winds blowing from 30 to 40 mph (just to give you a picture of what that night was like). So when Roderick Scott reached the foot of the driveway he announced that 911 had been called, that he had a gun and that the two remaining individuals should not move. Had they abided I'm sure they would both be alive today. Scott then saw James Cervini (Christopher's cousin) run toward the house and away from Christopher.

At this point Christopher ran towards Mr. Scott yelling something to the effect of "I'm going to get you" or "I'm going to get him" and started waving his arms towards Scott. So Christopher (who was nearly 17 years old) not only disregarded his request not to move but more importantly started running towards Roderick Scott in a threatening manner. It is at this point that Roderick Scott became justified to shoot (if this was Texas he could have shot Christopher just for attempting to steal some of his property earlier but pretty much every state allows you to defend yourself in this manner). The law code in New York is actually quite cumbersome but if you wade through it you will see that Mr. Scott was justified on multiple levels. Notice the following excerpt taken from Article 35 which governs Self Defense, this is Section 35.15 (I have bolded the relevant portions but if you aren't into legalese then just skip it):

> *Sec. 35.15 Justification; use of physical force in defense of a person.*
> *1. A person may, subject to the provisions of subdivision two, use physical force upon another person when and to the extent he reasonably believes such to be necessary to defend himself or a third person from what he reasonably believes to be the use or imminent use of unlawful physical force by such other person, unless:*
> *(a) The latter`s conduct was provoked by the actor himself with intent to cause physical injury to another person; or*
> *(b) The actor was the initial aggressor; except that in such case his use of physical force is nevertheless justifiable if he has withdrawn from the encounter and effectively communicated such withdrawal to such other person but the latter persists in continuing the incident by the use or threatened imminent use of unlawful physical force; or*
> *(c) The physical force involved is the product of a combat by agreement not specifically authorized by law.*
> *2. A person* **may not use deadly physical force upon another** *person under circumstances specified in subdivision one* ***unless:***
> *(a) He reasonably believes that such other person is using or about to use deadly physical force. Even in such case, however, the actor may not use deadly physical force if he knows that he can with complete safety as to himself and others avoid the necessity of so doing by retreating; except that he is under no duty to retreat if he is:*
> *(i) in his dwelling and not the initial aggressor; or*
> *(ii) a police officer or peace officer or a person assisting a police officer or a peace officer at the latter`s direction, acting pursuant to section 35.30; or*

*(b)* ***He reasonably believes that such other person is committing or attempting to commit a*** *kidnapping, forcible rape, forcible sodomy or* ***robbery****; or*
*(c) He reasonably believes that* ***such other person is committing or attempting to commit a burglary****, and the circumstances are such that the use of deadly physical force is authorized by subdivision three of section 35.20.*

Roderick Scott, in self-defense, fires twice at Cervini with one bullet going through the palm of Christopher Cervini and the second shot going through the rear part of his right armpit area. Of course **When Prosecutors Attack** these details get twisted and the Assistant DA Finocchino did exactly that in court on September 10, 2009 when she said that Mr. Scott shot the deceased "in the back". This would not be the last form of deception perpetrated by the prosecution in this case.

After the two shots Cervini is still approaching Scott but then collapses partially on the roadway so Roderick Scott does not need to fire a third shot. If you have ever shot a handgun you will know that you can fire off several shots in a short moment so stopping at two shots shows that Scott was in control of himself and not indiscriminately firing into the night air.

## After The Fact

Scott then leaned over Cervini and saw he had indeed been shot and posed no further threat. At this point Scott doubles back home and tells his significant other, Tracy, to call 911 again and tell them to send help. The prosecution tried desperately to paint Roderick Scott as some wannabe tough guy, meanwhile he is the background saying "oh my God, oh my God" showing that he did not in any way revel in this unfortunate teenage shooting death (however justified).

As the Felony Complaint below will show Mr. Scott then was interviewed by police at the scene (and this interview was recorded) and subsequently agreed to go to the Greece Police Department (Precinct Number 1) where he waived his rights and gave a videotaped statement[29].

---

[29] While I am here using these facts to support the innocence of Roderick Scott do not take this as an indication of what should be done in this type of situation. As a young child my father shrewdly put me under oath to never

We have submitted multiple FOIA (Freedom of Information Act) requests to the Greece PD and the Town of Greece all of which have been denied. Supposedly these records are sealed when a defendant is "exonerated" as they put it. Of course the state has not treated him as exonerated as we will get to a little later.

Later, Scott also waived immunity and testified before the Grand Jury. If I was the parent of the wayward teen that brought on his own untimely death I would certainly appreciate hearing from the shooter (of course they did not appreciate it but instead they maintain to this day that their child was this completely innocent angel that was just trying to go home but we will get to this a little later).

What much of the coverage of this case has failed to notice is that Mr. Scott's version of events was confirmed by two other witnesses that night (one of which was actually Brian Hopkins that confirmed at least part of his version of events).

The owner of 39 Baneberry Way gave a sworn statement in which he confirmed that the dome light was turned on in his vehicle thus confirming a very important detail, namely that these "teenagers" were criminals engaged in petty theft among other offenses and they had at least broken into the car at the scene of the shooting. Remember, Cervini was found to have marijuana in his system and I'm sure if the other culprits were tested they would have it in their systems as well.

---

speak to police without representation in such a situation. Certainly this type of cooperation didn't do anything for Mr. Scott in preventing this abusive prosecutorial attack.

State of New York — County of Monroe — Town of Greece

*The People of the State of New York*
against

| Roderick A. Scott | 05/27/67 |
| --- | --- |
| Defendant | DOB |

FELONY COMPLAINT
STATE OF NEW YORK
PENAL LAW
MURDER IN THE SECOND DEGREE
SECTION 125.25 SUB 2
CLASS A FELONY

THAT Sgts Michael Bihrle and Joseph Antinora Of the Greece Police Department
By this **FELONY COMPLAINT**, makes written accusation as follows:

THAT Roderick A. Scott Of ~~39~~ 58 Baneberry Way; Hilton, NY
did, on or about (time) 3:32 ☒AM ☐PM Date: April 4th ,20 09
at: 39 Baneberry Way , Town of Greece, New York, did
commit the offense of Murder in the Second Degree a Class A-1 Felony of Section 125.25 Sub 2 of the New York State Penal Law, in that he/she did, at the aforesaid time, date and place:

**COUNT ONE:**
**A person is guilty of Murder in the Second Degree when: under circumstances evincing a depraved indifference to human life, he recklessly engages in conduct which creates a grave risk of death to another person, and thereby causes the death of another person**

The facts upon which this **Felony Complaint** is based are as follows:

**On the above date and time, at the above location, the aforesaid defendant did under circumstances evincing a depraved indifference to human life, recklessly engage in conduct which created a grave risk of death to Christopher D. Cervini (DOB 12/04/91); to wit: above defendant did approach Christopher D. Cervini with a firearm in his hand, that being a Smith and Wesson .40 caliber automatic handgun and intentionally point and discharge said firearm at Christopher D. Cervini, striking Christopher D. Cervini at least two times causing the death of Christopher D. Cervini.**

**THE FOREGOING FACTUAL ALLEGATIONS ARE BASED UPON PERSONAL KNOWLEDGE OF THE COMPLAINANT** (and upon the information and belief, the sources of the complainant's information and belief being, the attached depositions which are attached herewith and made a part hereof).

**WHEREFORE,** the **Deponent** prays that the **Defendant** be dealt with in accordance with law.

**VERIFICATION BY SUBSCRIPTION & NOTICE, NYS PENAL LAW SECTION 210.45**
It is a Class A Misdemeanor under the laws of the State of New York, for a person, in and by a written instrument, to knowingly make a false statement, or to make a statement which such person does not believe to be true.

CR# 9020751 PCT# 1
IBM# 1021 SEX M RACE B
APP. DATE: 04/04/09
CO-DEF: ---

AFFIRMED UNDER PENALTY OF PERJURY, THIS:
04th DAY OF April (year) 2009
Sgt. [signature] #1021 [signature]
DEPONENT'S SIGNATURE

Please take notice that the People intend to offer at the trial of the defendant(s):
☒Evidence of a statement by the defendant made to a public servant : ☒ oral and recorded interview ☐ written (see attached)
Time: 6:32 AM/PM Date: 04/04/ 20 09 Place: GPD CID Interview Room #2
☐ Testimony identifying the defendant as the person who committed the offense charged, to be given by a witness who has previously identified the defendant as such. Type: ☐ photo ☐ show-up ☐ line-up
Time: ___ AM/PM Date: ___ 20 ___ Place: ___

(O L) GPD FORM # 24-00 REVISED 3/7/00

***Figure 17**: Felony Complaint Against Roderick Scott*

What I found most astounding and unforgiveable is the fact that the prosecution continued their attack even after the testimony of Brian Hopkins confirmed much of Mr. Scott's account of what occurred that night. First off I should mention that Mr. Hopkins is not the brightest bulb on the hardware store shelves. When Hopkins was asked where he lived in the April of the shooting he did not know the name of the street despite the fact that he had lived there for eight years (you can't make this stuff up). According to Hopkins, that night he went to James Cervini's house where the two Cervini cousins and Hopkins were drinking from a bottle of stolen gin. A toxicology report of Christopher Cervini later showed that he was legally drunk at the time of his death (along with marijuana and amphetamines in his system).

He even admitted to later going out to look for cigarettes with the Cervini boys. Hopkins goes on to relate that they were on Baneberry being loud (they would have to be loud enough to wake Scott who had fallen asleep on his downstairs couch that night) and that **they tried to get into several cars**. Brian was able to open one car and rummaged through the glove box **in search for smokes to steal**. Unsuccessful Hopkins says nothing was taken from the car they broke into. Even James Cervini admitted that Chris was leaning into a van after opening the door just before Scott made his presence known with a firm "Freeze. Don't move."

So, let's recap a bit before moving forward. I count four serious crimes committed by this gang (or at least Chris Cervini) prior to being confronted by Scott, namely underage drinking, underage smoking, attempted robbery *(but I'm sure this was not their first barbecue if you know what I mean)* and illicit drug use. Now you can debate about the merits and failings of the Drug War but the fact is that these "kids" were criminals that were caught in the commission of a crime (by anyone's standards) before Chris even chose to charge at Mr. Scott. By way of contrast Roderick Scott committed no crime. It is not a crime to own and bear a side arm. It is not a crime to investigate what you believe to be a crime (and what indisputably turned out to be a crime in progress even if you ignore Scott's testimony). Lastly it is not a crime to defend yourself when someone charges at you and threatens you.

But how do we actually know that this was self-defense? Well, besides the fact that Roderick Scott had absolutely no motive whatsoever to approach and murder a teenager he had never before met and putting aside the fact that Roderick Scott was approaching a group of undisputed criminals we know this was self-defense from the autopsy report. The autopsy report in conjunction with the Hopkins and Cervini testimony alone prove Mr. Scott's innocence to my satisfaction alone. Before getting into the details it may help you to first put this book down (I know it is hard to do) and go check out 39 Baneberry on Google Maps (go to maps.google.com and enter "loc: 39 Baneberry Way, Hilton, NY 14468" and then click on "Street View" when it comes up). This is where the shooting took place and you will see that these driveways are extra-long so that there was some distance initially between Scott who was on the street and the perpetrators that were by the van that was parked upslope and closer to the house.

Now, the other two boys ran essentially at the first site of Mr. Scott, apparently Hopkins saw Scott first (since he was the lookout) and so was the first to flee the scene of the crime (remember they were in the commission of a crime at the time). Christopher Cervini on the other hand must have charged at Scott and we know this for two important reasons. First, his body was found partially in the roadway[30] after the shooting. Second, there were no signs that the body was moved post-mortem.

While the cousin and accomplice, James Cervini, maintained that Chris didn't charge at Scott he is contradicted by his own testimony. If Chris was leaning into the van how else could he have made it all the way down on the roadway when he was shot if he had not been charging or at least approaching the armed Mr. Scott? Also, James Cervini is a person that should not be blindly taken at his word either. James at the "beautiful and gentle" age of 15 had been on probation twice for assisting in a burglary and for **holding a knife to the throat of a ten-year-old boy[31]** (supposedly the dispute involved marijuana). This may explain why Christopher charged at Roderick Scott since both Chris and James knew that if they got picked up for stealing from cars that the petty larceny would bring major consequences down on James. As Christopher's father was eager to point out his "kid" did not have a criminal record (this was the first time he got caught) so they would have lightly slapped him on the wrist and that would be the end of it.

---

[30] This was stated in the defense submission of a "Factual Background" and was not disputed by the state so this effectively becomes a fact stipulated by both sides.

[31] This is why we need to resist the tendency to think that every minor is some gentle and innocent child. If someone is holding a knife to a ten-year-olds throat then the age of the assailant becomes a completely irrelevant detail.

If the Monroe County Assistant District Attorney Julie Finocchino was really a proponent of justice above her own career she would have filed a motion to dismiss these charges after all these facts were entered into evidence and would not have sent this dog of a case to the jury. To be fair to Ms. Finocchino it is possible that the advantage of her own career was not the deciding factor and she is just incompetent (sheer stupidity could be blamed as well but it is not easy to pass the bar so I usually don't suspect that in a prosecutor). Either way it is clear that she was on the attack and was not going to be moved by exonerating evidence proving Mr. Scott's innocence. If not for cool headed disinterested jurors an innocent man would have been convicted.

Before moving on I should also mention that the fact that Christopher Cervini turned out to be unarmed is **a completely irrelevant part of the story**. Roderick Scott, again, had the right to arm himself and approach what he saw as (and what turned out to be) a crime in progress. When Chris charged at Mr. Scott indicating that he was going to "get" him Mr. Scott had the right to defend himself. Remember, even an unarmed man can do some considerable damage (as Treyvon Martin did to George Zimmerman) least of which is get control of the gun you are holding and turn it on you. That said, in Mr. Scott's case he had no idea in the dark of a cold April night if Cervini was armed or not. This is why it is a really bad idea to be breaking into cars or to be committing other crimes at night thinking that no one will see you rob their neighbors. It is also a very bad idea to charge at someone who is armed and ready to defend themselves.

I know that it is considered polite to tip toe around the memory of the deceased even if they were an unrepentant criminal. We have all sorts of superstitious sayings in our culture like that we should not "speak ill of the dead". These sentiments are neither biblical nor logical. We must speak ill of the dead. The entire subject of history is essentially speaking mostly ill of the dead. How can you discuss World War II without discussing all the evil perpetrated by Adolf Hitler? You cannot do so. Now Cervini was no Hitler, but he did violate the laws prohibiting him from drinking and smoking under the legal ages set for these activities. He did violate the laws prohibiting the possession and use of marijuana (and likely the laws prohibiting its purchase). He did break into cars, rummage through strangers personal affects and sought to steal their contents. All of these things are crimes. Then, after a night of breaking an array of laws, instead of waiting for police at the crime scene where he at least attempted to rob Mr. Scott's neighbor he chose instead to charge at Mr. Scott and thus brought about his own death.

It is for this reason that I must point a critical eye at his surviving parents as well. I know we have this instinct to sympathize with grieving parents but this sympathy can often interfere with our sense of justice and can have disastrous effects on the innocent lives of the surviving parties of such an unfortunate event. This sentiment is likely what drove Ms. Finocchino to push a case even after the facts clearly demonstrated Mr. Scott's innocence. Again had the Jury not viewed the facts objectively an innocent man would have been imprisoned.

The first time I saw the post-trial interview with the Cervini parents I just felt badly for them (as a father I cannot imagine the pain of losing a child under any circumstances). Then after reviewing the details of the case and then re-watching the interview I am aghast that the urge to justify your child's criminal behavior could be so strong to overshadow your sense of justice and reason. I hope to never have to be in their unfortunate position. If I did find myself in that unfortunate position, though, I would hope that I would not pursue the persecution of an innocent shooter. Instead, the pony-tail toting father tells the press that his son was a good kid that had never gotten into any trouble (meaning he had not yet been caught) and that somehow Roderick Scott was lying about Chris having threatened him (even though again he was shot at the foot of the driveway showing that he had been charging toward Scott). He wasn't there of course but no reporter is going to put a grieving parent under any kind of scrutiny. We have documented an array of crimes committed by Christopher Cervini but that doesn't mean anything to his parents.

I grew up in New York around many such parents that would continually make excuses for their children. Even after his son's own actions led to his own death this father would rather blame an innocent concerned neighbor than own up to the fact that their son was a criminal plain and simple. It is unfortunate that he didn't grow up in time to straighten up (or conversely to get caught for his pattern of breaking the law). If this were my child I would be hanging my head in shame and be saying that I should have done more to keep him from using illicit drugs. The father also tells the press "and the message is that we can all go out and get guns and shoot anyone that we feel is threatening us." To that I would say: YES, that's why people buy handguns. Only it has nothing to do with our 'feelings' but if someone is caught in the commission of a crime and charges at you (as was the case here) you definitely can use your sidearm to defend yourself if you are fortunate enough to be armed at the time.

The mother was even worse but of course parents get a pass to say all sorts of incorrect things to the press. She told the press that "all he wanted to do was go home" when in fact he wasn't just on a stroll home but was robbing Mr. Scott's neighbors. She also said that he said "I'm just a kid" and Scott "kept shooting". Of course only two shots were fired in quick succession.

Maybe I'm from another planet but I don't feel the need to put reason and logic aside just because someone has lost a child. If I take the time to think about it then it starts to bother me that the mother of a deceased criminal goes on about how her son was "a beautiful and sweet child". Remember we have to live in a world with the children of parents like the Cervini parents. These parents make every excuse under the sun to excuse their child's behavior so it is no wonder at the young age of 16 or 17 that Christopher Cervini was already drinking, smoking, toking, and robbing. That is not what I call "sweet" or "beautiful" and if these parents weren't in a pattern of making excuses for their child (or if they just knew where their kid was in the middle of the night) their son might be alive today. I agree that I am speculating a bit and it is possible that these were great parents that just had an out of control child (but the fact that they do not own up to that fact leads me to doubt that very much)

This was indeed a tragedy but not one perpetrated by Mr. Scott. No one wants to be viewed as attacking the bereaved and at the same time no parent wants to come to terms with their bad parenting. These two factors combine to wreak havoc on innocent people's lives as it did for OJ Simpson, Roderick Scott and George Zimmerman (as we will get to later). In light of that I hope you take this as necessary dialogue and not just as insensitive bantering because when there is a shooting death everyone's reputation is like eggs you are juggling and you just can't keep them all in the air – some of them are going to hit the ground and since we have this superstitious "don't speak ill of the dead" theology in this country all too often the surviving innocent shooter is the one who's life is ripped apart by the media and government. It is just a cold hard fact that when there is a shooting death the shooter and the deceased can't both have been acting honorably (and every dead man can't be a saint so at least one person is at fault). Actually in many cases both parties are at fault, as in the case of drug deals gone south, but when the two parties have no personal or business connection to each other usually one person is at fault. I know in both cases in this volume I have sided with the shooter but often the shooter is the guilty party in such an encounter (as is the case with serial killers) but in isolated encounters like the Roderick Scott and George Zimmerman cases it is very difficult to establish an alternate theory of motive from what the shooters themselves state.

Try and think about this logically: what possible motive would Roderick Scott have for chasing down a perfectly innocent white teen and shooting him to death for no reason? It is not as if police found stacks of anti-white racist literature in his house. Roderick wasn't some Tribu Ka member or even a Nation of Islam adherent. Don't misunderstand me: I'm not saying that everyone in those organizations is a racist murderer, not by a long shot. But Roderick Scott was a pretty stable individual who supported six kids and had been at the same job for as long as Christopher Cervini had been alive. Without any motive (or indication of being a serial killer) Roderick Scott must be given the benefit of the doubt which he was by a Jury of his peers. Of course, even without his testimony the autopsy plus the testimony of the surviving car thieves is enough to exonerate him and we should all be thankful that the Jury saw it that way as well.

So, how does the State deal with the fact that they have been persecuting an innocent man? Do they come to terms with this during the trial and dismiss the charges? Almost never in most cases and really never when they have sunk their teeth into a high profile case that could make their career. Even the Roderick Scott case that didn't make national news was still a huge case for ADA Finocchino since it was being regularly covered on the local news stations. Rather than admit that she had leveled charges against an innocent man she instead pushed forward with her prosecution and sent this joke of a case to the Jury.

Okay, so what about after the Jury exonerated and set free this man who by that point had his life turned upside down by the State? Surely, the prosecutors would give a statement praising the jury system and make a comment about how they were an advocate for the surviving Cervini family members but that ultimately these decisions are left to dispassionate, disinterested Jurors for a reason. Not even close. Notice what Ms. Finocchino had to say after the verdict came out:

> *"I just hope it's not a message to this community... that you have the right to shoot an unarmed 17-year-old* ***kid for breaking into a car.*** *"* (Emphasis ours)

This kind of stuff makes me crazy! Roderick Scott didn't execute the misguided teen for breaking into a car, he shot him because this boozed up, drugged up teen reacted to getting caught burglarizing a car by **charging at Mr. Scott in a threatening manner** (in the dark of night nonetheless).

Remember that according to Hopkins they were making quite a bit of noise that April night. Therefore, Roderick Scott had no idea if neighbors were looking on from the safety of their homes at this point. Why on earth would this man just execute a kid simply for breaking into a car? It simply did not happen. I invite you to find the video interviews with him on Youtube and make up your own mind if this was some murderous thug out for innocent blood or if this was a reasonable person just trying to protect his neighborhood and ultimately himself.

Conversely, when you see the parents interviewed you start to get a window into the upbringing of the deceased. The fact that they were breaking into cars that night was not disputed in anyway during the Roderick Scott trial. Even so, the Cervini father did not get the right message from the trial. Remember he stated: "and the message is that we can all go out and get guns and shoot anyone that we feel is threatening us." **The real message** to take away from this case is that parents should do everything in their power to **make sure their kids aren't out using drugs, getting drunk and trying to steal things from people's cars** and if they are unable to reign in their kids the consequences can be fatal.

Of course Roderick Scott did not shoot Chris Cervini for any of those reasons in and of themselves but all of that criminal behavior and association is what led Cervini to be in that high tension situation where a wrong decision on his part cost him his life.

One aspect of this case that I was impressed with is how Roderick Scott was not embittered by this entire ordeal. His response after the verdict was that "I feel that justice was served today" and he went on to state that he regrets that someone had to lose his life in the night in question. He displayed much more sympathy than I would for a family that raised a criminal and after the fact chose to ignore the fact that their drunken drug-using thief of a son tried to attack Mr. Scott that dark and cold April night.

His lawyer was also diplomatic but his comments were much more to the point: "I just want to say that I hope this case sends a message to families out there **to watch their kids, to know where they are and what they are doing.**" (Emphasis Ours)

Amen to that.

## Roderick Scott: Black Zimmerman or Not?

Well, like I stated before no two cases are exactly the same but things don't need to be exactly the same to make a corollary between them. In fact, one effective tool in public speaking is to make use of illustrations. Often times illustrations will be used to just highlight a single point of comparison, like the futility of rowing with one paddle or pushing a giant boulder up a hill that you know will roll back down before you get to the top. Now chances are that you will never give a speech on moving rocks or even rowing techniques but these illustrations can be effective because they help to illustrate a single point of comparison in a very visual format that is easy to remember and makes the point. So with regard to the similarities between the Roderick Scott case and the Zimmerman case there are many but some important distinctions. Take note of the following table that compares several aspects of this case:

| Comparison Point | Roderick Scott | George Zimmerman |
|---|---|---|
| Race | Black | White (Latin) |
| Age[32] | 42 | 28 |
| Race of Shot Person | White | Black |
| Age of Shot Person | 16 | 17 |
| Subsequent Arrest | Immediate | 45 Days After |
| Shooter Injured? | No | Yes |
| Cross Racial Shooting? | Yes | Yes |
| Gun Legally Owned? | Yes | Yes |
| Shooter Active in Neighborhood Watch? | Yes | Yes |
| Self-Defense Evident? | Yes | Yes |
| Shooter Approached on Suspicion of Criminal Activity? | Yes | Yes |
| Deceased Used Illicit Drugs? | Yes | Yes |
| Deceased Had a Documented Violent Background? | No | Yes |
| 911 Was Called By Shooter? | Yes | Yes |
| Deceased Had a Documented History of Dealing Drugs? | No | Yes |
| National Media Outrage? | No | Yes |
| Prosecutors Ignored Exonerating Evidence? | Yes | Yes |
| Race Based Prosecution? | Maybe[33] | Yes |
| Found Not Guilty? | Yes | Yes |

[32] This refers to the age of the shooter at the time of the shooting in question.
[33] I say maybe because in the Roderick Scott case the shooter was black and both Cervini and the prosecutor were Italian (coming from New York this just raises an eyebrow). That said I agree with Bill Cosby: "See this racial stuff goes into a whole bunch of discussion which has **stuff that you can't prove**."

So I hope if nothing else you can see from the table that there are some important differences between the cases and some very significant similarities. Some of the differences are pretty obvious such as the fact that in the Roderick Scott case the races are reversed (black self-defense shooter and white teenager shot). Normally I try to avoid making meaningless racial distinctions since I'm just so tired of hearing about this hackneyed issue. However, it was repeated ad nausea in the mainstream media that *'if the races were reversed in the Zimmerman case and the shooter were black he would have been convicted'* so on that basis I think it is valid to bring up the Roderick Scott case to prove that this simply is not true (and truth be told these things are said for the purpose of furthering the racial divide in this country) since indeed Mr. Scott was exonerated.

That said, one important difference that is cited by detractors is that while **Mr. Scott was arrested immediately** after the shooting (that night) it took **about 6 weeks and national pressure to get Zimmerman arrested.** While that is technically true it glosses over the fact that Zimmerman was **visibly beaten up** and thus bore the physical evidence of needing to defend himself on his person. Roderick Scott was not physically harmed by his encounter with Christopher Cervini and thus it is more understandable that police would make an arrest and sort out the details after the fact. What is egregious, in the Roderick Scott case, is that when the dust settled and everyone had an opportunity to sleep on the facts available that the prosecutors chose to move forward with this baseless legal attack on Mr. Scott (all the way to sending this dog of a case to the Jury).

Remember that most of the mainstream media is simply choosing to ignore the similarities between the George Zimmerman and Roderick Scott cases and the only Martin supporters really digging into this comparison (in an attempt to refute the similarities) seem to be bloggers and YouTube video-bloggers. Another "important" difference they hit on is that Roderick Scott approached the teens that were already in the commission of a crime (robbing from cars) whereas Trayvon Martin had not committed any crime at the time that Zimmerman approached him. From a legal perspective this would on its face be considered a difference without a distinction. On a public street it is legal for anyone (that does not have a restraining order against them) to approach any other individual and start asking them questions. Now Martin didn't have to answer any of Zimmerman's questions, he could have simply kept walking or stayed where he was or done anything else besides getting violent and beating up Zimmerman. Remember that besides the final defensive gun shot that Martin's body sustained absolutely no bruises from his encounter with Zimmerman (meaning that the only one being beaten up prior to the gunshot was Zimmerman) so **this was not a "fight"** as some have chosen to brand it **but in fact a beating**, plain and simple!

That said the fact remains that both Roderick Scott and George Zimmerman approached the deceased on suspicion of criminal activity. We have clearly established that the Cervini boys and Brian Hopkins were engaged in several criminal acts prior to their encounter with Roderick Scott. Was Trayvon Martin engaged in criminal activity at the time George Zimmerman approached him (even though we have already established that this detail is legally irrelevant)? We will get into this more in the next chapter but the short answer is: yes!

Besides being under the influence of marijuana (he had 1.5 ng/mL in his system at the time of death – enough to indicate he had just gotten high within the previous 8 hours) which is a crime generally covered under "Public Intoxication", Martin was also peering into homes and trespassing in what looked to George Zimmerman like someone casing a house for a robbery (in violation of privacy and trespassing laws but would still not be considered attempted robbery unless he touched a window or door attempting to gain entry according to our legal consultant). Zimmerman had no way of knowing at the time that Martin actually had a history of robbery (or for that matter drug dealing) and had been found at school to have stolen jewelry in his backpack which we will get into more in the next chapter.

## Verdict

So to answer the question of if Roderick Scott is the 'Black Zimmerman' I would say: yes, to the extent that two cases can be similar that they these two are analogous. An armed man of one race, approaches another man[34] of a different race whom he suspects of

[34] And yes I consider these thieving, smoking, drug-using teenagers "boys" to be men. In Jewish culture a teenage boy is considered a man and in most

criminal activity, the man approached responds violently and the armed man defends himself with his handgun.

Also, in terms of being an answer to the "what would have happened if the races were reversed" question I would say that the answer is simply: Roderick Scott. Unfortunately, all races are subject to mindless prosecutorial attacks.

It is true that the evidence proving that Zimmerman was acting in self-defense is stronger than that used to exonerate Mr. Scott in the sense that it included forensic evidence (proving Martin had been beating Zimmerman) and fortunately there were eye-witnesses to confirm his account. On the other hand, the evidence that exonerated Roderick Scott was circumstantial in nature but it was still very strong circumstantial evidence leaving no reasonable alternative to Roderick's own account. The juries in both cases examined the evidence put before them and really had no choice but to exonerate both men.

Imagine for a moment that it was you, that you were the concerned neighbor investigating what you thought to be criminal behavior. Imagine that you were attacked (or about to be attacked) but you were able to defend yourself with your sidearm. Then imagine that the state turns on you and ignores every piece of evidence that should easily exonerate you. This is not some extraterrestrial science fiction; unfortunately this is exactly what happens **When Prosecutors Attack!**

---

traditional economies by their ages they have already taken on their fathers trade and is able to start supporting himself (this 18 business is completely arbitrary)

# UNIT THREE: GEORGE ZIMMERMAN

# **GEORGE ZIMMERMAN**: THE WHITE RODERICK SCOTT

With all the comparisons being made to the Roderick Scott case the fact that the Roderick Scott case came several years before the Zimmerman case gets lost. If anything Zimmerman is the white Roderick Scott (and not the other way around). So here rather than focus on the similarities we can highlight some important differences between how these cases were handled by the state and the media alike.

First of all it has become popular for Fox News commentators to make the claim that the media is unfairly bent against white shooters and that only whites get this treatment. This is a gross simplification of what actually happens and if nothing else I think our coverage of the OJ Simpson case in this volume should be proof of that. Yes, the media was jumping at the opportunity to turn this very ordinary case into a national circus to further the racial divide in the United States (and to some degree globally). However, the OJ Simpson case showed how the government-media complex will turn on whomever it chooses, regardless of race.

Remember, too, that furthering the racial divide for political purposes was only part of the narrative being pushed. This is just as much about citizens being armed in general as it was about white and black. The government (and some might say 'especially *this* government' in reference to the Obama administration) does not want anyone armed that is not directly on its payroll (like police, SWAT, DHS, etc.)[35]

Why wasn't the Roderick Scott case made into a national concern? Well like the Zimmerman case this was just a local self-defense shooting that really does not merit a national discussion. That said imagine if the media did make the Roderick Scott case into a national debacle. What would the angle be? Well, for once you would have to show a black man legally exercising his second amendment rights. This is a huge anathema to the mainstream media. Often the media (especially TV and print newspapers) is branded as being "liberal" but it really goes much deeper than even that. What the media is really bent on is not getting the whole country into one political party but rather to keep the country divided into two camps. CNN and MSNBC can pretend to be liberal (even though they implicitly endorse almost every military action especially if a democrat is president) and Fox News can pretend to be conservative (even though they almost never cover stories of citizens legally using guns to save their life or the lives of others even though there are more than enough such cases to run a weekly special). The job of these two sides is to keep people divided into two opposing camps and prop up the illusion that there is any significant difference between the parties (even though both parties continue to run up the national debt, mushroom the size of government and engage in a never ending string of foreign military conflicts).

Instead of showing blacks legally using guns for good (which happens quite frequently) blacks are only connected to guns in a criminal context on television. So, every year law abiding blacks become less and less likely to exercise their second amendment rights. A few blacks end up using guns in the commission of crimes (as the media is

[35] It is darkly humorous how average Americans stocking up on ammo that may not be available in the future are being branded as crazy "preppers" while the government is amassing more ammunition than it has since the advent of gun powder. The DHS has by itself recently stocked enough ammunition to shoot every inhabitant of the United States seven times each (or put another way by Iraq War standards they have enough ammunition at this very moment to conduct a 20 year domestic conflict). For this reason Obama is sometimes dubbed the "Prepper-in-chief" (especially by gun owners that are simply following the example set by the DHS and stocking up for their own family).

happy to report) but the vast majority (who of course are law abiding) end up taking an anti-second amendment attitude. What would happen if the media constantly reported stories of blacks using guns to legally defend themselves or others? Well, then more of them might start to view gun ownership as a part of a respectable man's life. Of course, legal gun ownership tends to lead to more conservative values. Such a trend might bring conservatives and blacks together in a way that has only seemed to occur in about 4% of the black community (who are usually very religious and pro-life).

I do not consider myself to be a political person in the sense that I don't vote nor do I have faith in the political systems of the world today. However, some political points must be touched on simply to lay the groundwork for understanding why there was such a huge difference between the level of the media's interest in the Roderick Scott case and the George Zimmerman trial.

Imagine if someone had asked the question, during the limited coverage of the Roderick Scott case, of: "if the races were reversed what would have been the outcome?"

Some may have said that a white man defending himself would never have been prosecuted like Roderick Scott was. In fact, Mr. Scott's own lawyer, John Parrinello, said as much in the "Factual Background" he submitted to the court in Roderick's behalf. He said *"I truly believe* ***if Scott were not black and the deceased white****, there would have been no immediate arrest for murder and perhaps a complete investigation which would have indicted Mr. Scott".*

Unfortunately, his skilled lawyer was dead wrong in this case. George Zimmerman shows that a prosecutor ("special" or otherwise) will go after anyone of any race, especially on high profile cases that offer any prospect of a career boost (remember even though Roderick Scott didn't make national news it was still a "high profile" case for the otherwise sleepy Town of Greece). Of course many would point to the fact that Zimmerman wasn't immediately arrested but remember that, unlike Mr. Scott, George Zimmerman was wearing his evidence of self-defense all over his body in the form of bruises, cuts, a broken nose and his own blood.

To Parrinello's credit, however, no one could have predicted that the Federal government would have financed rallies against a private citizen as they did against George Zimmerman. Many people have wondered why the George Zimmerman case was made into a national story when thousands of actual murders go largely unnoticed each year. The media was partly to blame but it is clear now that even the Federal government was fanning the divisive fire brewing against Mr. Zimmerman. The **Department of Justice's** (DOJ) CRS group actually **laid out the money to organize the protests against George Zimmerman**. One would think that this alone would be an impeachable offense. Remember that the ignorance and hatred that was promulgated in these anti-Zimmerman rallies has led to **no less than six murders** of people displaying any sort of support for George Zimmerman (in one case two brothers were murdered simply for having a "FREE ZIMMERMAN" bumper sticker).[36]

Thanks to the Judicial Watch there have been a series of successful FOIA[37] requests and thankfully much of the DOJ's support of these rallies has come out. The total figure of the amount of support the DOJ has given towards demonizing this private citizen is unclear. The Judicial Watch has only been given 222 pages of documents and from that have established the following:

- March 25 – 27, 2012, CRS spent **$674.14** upon being "deployed to Sanford, FL, to work **marches**, demonstrations, and **rallies** related to the shooting and death of an African-American teen by a neighborhood watch captain."
- March 25 – 28, 2012, CRS spent **$1,142.84** "in Sanford, FL to work marches, demonstrations, and rallies related to the shooting and death of an African-American teen by a neighborhood watch captain."
- March 30 – April 1, 2012, CRS spent **$892.55** in Sanford, FL "to provide interregional **support for protest deployment** in Florida."

[36] Not to mention that our own researcher, Sundance, had his car **set on fire while it was sitting in a Police Department PARKING LOT** while he was on the beat campaigning to get the stolen jewelry that was found on Trayvon Martin returned to its rightful owners (since it was just sitting in a police locker despite it matching the items stolen in a burglary reported near Martin's high school).

[37] Freedom of Information Act

- March 30 – April 1, 2012, CRS spent an additional **$751.60** in Sanford, FL "to provide technical assistance to the City of Sanford, **event organizers**, and law enforcement agencies for the march and rally on March 31."
- April 3 – 12, 2012, CRS spent **$1,307.40** in Sanford, FL "to provide technical assistance, conciliation, and onsite mediation during **demonstrations** planned in Sanford."
- April 11 – 12, 2012, CRS spent **$552.35** in Sanford, FL "to **provide technical assistance** for the preparation of possible **marches and rallies** related to the fatal shooting of a 17 year old African American male."

These may seem like small amounts but this is just what Judicial Watch has been able to obtain. If you have never tried to submit a FOIA request to a government agency about a sensitive matter you may not appreciate that it is like pulling teeth. For this volume **we have submitted thirteen FOIA requests** and have received little more than "denied" back in most cases (with the exception of one highly ambiguous letter from the DEA that they might get back to us at some point but to more or less not hold our breath). So, these findings should be viewed like cockroaches: for every one you do see there are likely dozens you don't see. But the fact that the State of Florida proceeded with this prosecution even after the lead investigator said he believed Zimmerman's version of the events that night (because they matched the rest of the facts in the case), the Sanford Police Chief Bill Lee refused to charge Zimmerman with any crime (a stand he was later fired for taking) and the local State Attorney Norm Wolfinger decided that there was insufficient evidence to convict Geroge Zimmerman of manslaughter should tell you that **this prosecution was propelled for purely political reasons**.

The governor had to bring in a prosecutor from another district that was willing to prosecute any defendant with a pulse, namely Angela Corey a woman with a checkered history all her own. Since she was the main prosecutor in this case let's look a bit into her past (and we'll even touch on her little bald sidekick, Bernie de la Rionda).

## Angela Corey's Abuse of Power

Before even getting to the abuses of prosecutorial power I can't help but relate what many are calling the **Taxpayer Pension Fund Scandal** which implicates both Angela Corey and Bernie de la Rionda (the prosecutors in the Martin case). Essentially, State Attorneys in the state of Florida are given an office budget that they can spend nearly completely at their own discretion (but of course the purpose of the funds is to run their offices). Both of the Martin case prosecutors were found to have diverted much of their office budgets towards padding their already generous pension retirement accounts. According to Florida law this is technically legal (however sleazy it may appear) and Angela Corey, in her signature arrogant tone, responded to criticism on this point by saying *"whatever the law allows for career prosecutors is what we intend to do".* I'm always amazed at how legitimate sounding corrupt officials can make themselves sound.

*Figure 18: The Face of Prosecutorial Abuse of Power*

Photo: Associated Press

This was by no means small change, in fact back in February reports came out that Angela Corey approved using $342,000 in taxpayer money to upgrade pensions for herself and Bernie de la Rionda (the prosecutor who blocked a responsible whistleblower that we will get into shortly).

Getting back to her actual work as a prosecutor, any examination of Angela Corey's track record will show that she has a "lock up the kids and throw away the key" attitude toward juvenile crime. Now I know a lot of my readers will be strong law and order types and I respect that. Certainly the other end of that spectrum, namely the "lets blame the criminal's childhood instead of the criminal" crowd, is a ridiculous attitude but charging children as adults causes all sorts of problems. Primarily, it means that juveniles are now raised in adult prisons and as a result have a much higher likelihood of recidivism. In 2009 there was an analysis conducted by the University of Texas at Austin regarding the practice of trying children as adults. The authors of the study wrote:

> *"The practice of treating children as adults for criminal justice purposes also poses serious risk to the individual child. The research* ***unequivocally shows that children prosecuted as adults are more likely to re-offend*** *and to pose a threat to society."*

However, Angela Corey made a regular practice of trying children as adults. One case that was particular egregious was **Florida V. Cristian Fernandez** wherein a boy, although disturbed and needing punishment, was being tried as an adult for first-degree murder. Fernandez was ten years at the time of his younger brother's death. He was left at home alone with his younger two year old brother who he slammed against a bookshelf and otherwise rough housed with. When the mother came home she saw that the younger child had sustained an injury to his head that seemed serious. She then looked online for home remedies, then did her banking, watched some YouTube videos and eventually after 8 hours or so brought him to the emergency room where he eventually died and she was told they could have done something had she brought him in earlier. I'm sure hearing that is a horror the mother (who had her first child when she was only 12 years old herself) will have to live with for the rest of her life. Getting back to Cristian, he is certainly a disturbed young child who needs a mixture of punishment and treatment. Again, not to use the perpetrators childhood to water down their crime (although this does hold a little more weight when the perpetrator is still a child) but Cristian himself was also a legitimate victim himself, having been found earlier by police – at the age of two – to be wandering the streets of Florida while his grandmother who was supposed to be watching him was busy getting high on crack.

In another case a **legitimately abused wife**, Marissa Alexander, fired a warning shot into the living room wall to prevent her husband from beating her. Angela Corey charged Marissa with **all sorts of questionable charges** due to the incident including "endangering a minor" because her kids were nearby while it happened. See, if you are a man being beaten severely by a younger man (or a nearly six foot tall "child") you are just supposed to sit there and take it. Also, if you are an abused woman who is about to be attacked again and is thinking of standing up for yourself this time, well according to Angela Corey you better not do so with a gun *(because most abused women are physically equal to their abusive male counterparts so that should work out fine).*

The point of all this is just to say that Angela Corey has been eager to make her cases regardless of who was being prosecuted and what the circumstances were that surrounded the cases she pursued. Also, it just **showcases how disingenuous she was being** when she would refer to the fallen Trayvon as a "child". So, let's get this straight: Trayvon Martin who was 5'11" (towering over George Zimmerman who is a mere 5'7"), 17 years old, and was on top of George Zimmerman beating him senseless was just a child but an 11 year old that rough houses with their toddler brother and injures him in a way that would not have been fatal except for the neglect of the mother is **a full grown adult murderer?**

If we are going to listen to State Attorney Corey this is the type of double think we have to swallow. But Angela Corey will never be interviewed in this fashion. Prosecutors are free to abuse their power and conveniently take contradicting positions when it is convenient for their current prosecution (not to mention their careers).

This is why it concerns me so deeply that we have gone from a society where we as jurors used to reject charges made by the state against our fellow citizens 25% of the time to a country where we shut down prosecutors only 7% of the time[38].

That said, I do not consider myself an expert on the Cristian Fernandez or Marissa Alexander cases and I invite you to look into both of them yourself. Really though, her **prosecutorial overreach** in her previous cases and even the **Taxpayer Pension Fund Scandal** are nothing compared to how whistleblowers were handled in the Trayvon Martin case.

## Operation Blow-up the Whistleblowers

What we are about to address in this section should be viewed as totally normal and not at all shocking if we were discussing something that occurred in the 1970's era Soviet Union. Unfortunately, this **suppression of key evidence** and retaliation against **legitimate whistleblowing** is something that has just recently occurred in this country (and like cockroaches must represent dozens if not hundreds of similar instances of which we are unaware).

**Ben Kruidbos was the IT director** for Florida's State Attorneys' Office (SAO). He retrieved evidence from Trayvon's phone, including a picture of a hand holding a gun and another of a gun on a bed. He was also able **to retrieve text messages about drug dealing** and pictures of Marijuana plants from the same phone.

He **put his info in a report** and gave it to Assistant State Attorney Bernie de la Rionda (Angela Corey's bald sidekick[39]). According to Kruidbos, de la Rionda gave mixed signals about turning info over to Zimmerman's lawyers which he ultimately failed to do.

---

[38] This is just another way to look at the numbers I brought out in the first chapter of this volume, that since 1972 the conviction rate has soared from 75% to roughly 93%.

[39] No offense to my bald readers but I find that the vivid imagery helps when trying to sort through all of these names especially in written form.

In May, **months after giving his report** to de la Rionda, Kruidbos contacted Wesley White. White is a retired Florida prosecutor who now has his own private practice. White gave all of this previously withheld information to the Zimmerman's attorneys. Did the prosecution ever give a legitimate reason for **withholding this key information?** Certainly not! If they had to be honest they would have to answer as did Jim Carry's character in the film **"Liar Liar"** where he honestly admitted that his only reason for objecting was: **"because it is devastating to my case!"**

Kruidbos later **testified at a June 6th pre-trial hearing** that he discovered the photos after using software to analyze the raw data from Martin's phone. Then he put it all in a report and turned it over to Assistant State Attorney Bernie de la Rionda. Most importantly, he testified that the SAO had concealed key evidence from Zimmerman's lawyers which of course why he needed to turn to external whistleblowing (since he had exhausted his options internally). *In the following flowchart you can see the sequence of events laid out and the parties involved.*

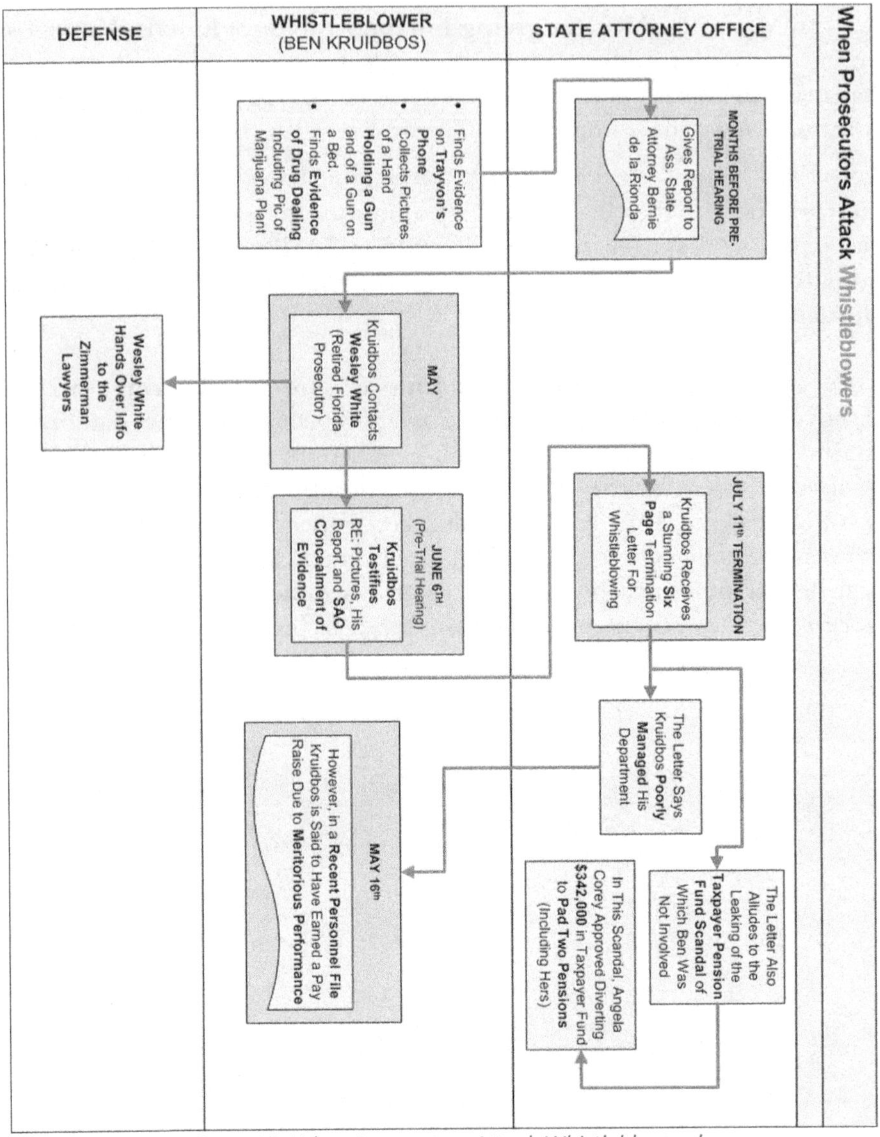


***Figure 19**: When Prosecutors Attack Whistleblowers!*

Shortly after his testimony Kruidbos received a six page termination letter from the SAO dated July 11th. It was signed by SAO Managing Director, Cheryl R. Peek. The letter, dated July 11, states:

> *"It has come to our attention that you* ***violated numerous State Attorney's Office (SAO) policies*** *and procedures and have engaged in deliberate misconduct that is especially egregious in light of your position as Director of Information Technology (IT)."*

In other words it is the **policy of the SAO to withhold key evidence** and for the IT Director to become complicit in this concealment and not report it outside of the department? The letter goes on with its vitriol:

> *"Your egregious lack of regard for the sensitive nature of the information handled by this office is completely abhorrent. You have proven to be completely untrustworthy. Because of your deliberate, willful and unscrupulous actions,* ***you can never again be trusted to step foot in this office****".*

This was not at all a composed business letter; you can tell that they are pretty heated up over having their misconduct exposed. The letter alleges that Kruidbos' intent *"was not* ***pursuant to any pure motive*** *or genuine concern."*

Yes, they went there! An office **that withheld exculpatory evidence** month after month and then decides to fire the one man that blows the whistle on their misconduct has the audacity to disparage the purity of the whistleblowers motives!!!!! **What were <u>their</u> motives in concealing key evidence** that contradicted their own fabricated narrative that Trayvon Martin was an innocent law-abiding child?

> *"Your feigned and spurious claim of possible liability was nothing more than shameful manipulation in a shallow, but obvious, attempt* ***to cloak yourself in the protection of the whistleblower law****"*

This is where it gets scary. They are here referencing the Florida statute that bars retaliation against state employees who disclose protected information. Most government agencies and large companies have policies that protect whistleblowers. If you have ever worked for Fortune 100 company or a government agency you know that one HR policy that gets drilled into your head is that you will not have to suffer retaliation for reporting wrongdoing within your department. Without such protection for a whistleblower then every employee would feel too intimidated to come forward when they see corruption within the ranks of management.

If the state starts demonizing individuals that are relying on the protection of these anti-retaliatory whistleblower provisions (as Ms. Peek has done in Kruidbos' termination letter) then this will have an enormous chilling effect as I'm sure his termination has had within the Florida State government or at least within the SAO.

Also, if Ben Kruidbos is not **a legitimate whistleblower then who is?** We are not talking about him divulging some internal conversation about a case where simple strategy was discussed. We are talking about **solid techno-forensic evidence** about the deceased in an ongoing murder trial! We are talking about evidence that **he waited months for his department to turn over** to the defense (which they were obligated to do immediately – certainly within 48 hours or one business day, whichever came later to be reasonable). Lastly we are talking about evidence that **directly contradicts** the picture the prosecution was painting of the deceased. Kruidbos testified that Martin's cell phone contained images of himself blowing smoke, various images of marijuana and marijuana plants, pictures of guns and even deleted text messages regarding a transaction for a firearm and that all this information hadn't been given to Zimmerman's defense team. We can't forget that the prosecution's case depended on getting the jury to disbelieve any notion that Zimmerman had a legitimate reason to suspect Martin of criminal activity in the first place (even though this detail is completely legally irrelevant and private citizen can approach and speak with any other private citizen on the street – unless a restraining order is in place – and ask them questions).

For the prosecution to be successful they needed to counter the **overwhelming eyewitness and forensic evidence that Martin was the one brutalizing Zimmerman** before the gunshot with the idea that Martin was this innocent respectable honor student. To bolster this claim Martin supporters point to the a claim that Trayvon Martin had a 3.7 GPA and a full scholarship to college (keep in mind that the former is deeply in question since his academic records have not been released and the latter is almost certainly untrue since he had just turned 17 making it highly unlikely that he had even visited or applied to any colleges) which is really meaningless anyhow when you attend one of the worst failing public schools in a state that has a very low ranking in terms of educaiton[40]. I have worked with several valedictorians from these types of schools and they can hardly complete comprehensible sentences.

Of course, someone can be a drug dealing drop out and it would have no bearing on the guilt of a shooter in and of itself. However when evidence of self-defense is countered by a false picture of a "good" (meaning law abiding and non-violent) kid that couldn't possibly have attacked Zimmerman then this information becomes relevant. When the prosecution asks a jury to put aside eyewitness testimony that Martin was on top of Zimmerman and brutalizing him and to put aside forensic evidence showing that Martin had not sustained injury prior to being shot because you say he was a good child and was non-violent then evidence to the contrary become vitally relevant.

Really, at this point the prosecution should not only have handed this information over to the defense but should have dropped the charges. Remember this is a case in which even the Sanford Police did not want to make an arrest and the assigned State Attorney did not think there was sufficient evidence and refused to press charges!

So I think we can agree that **When Prosecutors Attack** they can turn on any race of man when they have a career making case brewing. In Roderick Scott's case he didn't have the national media and Federal government on a campaign against him but he didn't have the immediate physical evidence on his person of having had his life threatened so his initial arrest is somewhat understandable. Even so, the facts leading up to Roderick's prosecution consistently came out in his favor which would have caused a decent prosecutor to drop the charges or even keep them for pressing charges in the first place. In the Zimmerman case you almost had the reverse (or more accurately the inverse) where initially the police and prosecution jumped the right way because exculpatory evidence was immediately available and abundant. It should have ended there except for the fact that the national media and the Federal government were out for blood and without too much effort were able to coax hordes of angry (and at least on six fatal

[40] Florida consistently ranks in the bottom 25 percent in national surveys and average test-score rankings. See: *Matus, Ron, (6 March 2005). "Schools still rank near the bottom", St. Petersburg Times.*

occasions violent) and confused protesters to support a baseless prosecution.

Did Roderick Scott shoot and ultimately kill Christopher Cervini because he was white? The very thought is preposterous. Did Zimmerman approach Trayvon Martin because of his skin color? This idea is as ridiculous as it is ultimately irrelevant. We touched on this a bit in our chapter focusing on race but it bears addressing once more. Roderick Scott lived in a relatively white part of New York and never exhibited any anti-white hatred (which is part of the reason we have no reason to interject race into that self-defense case). By the same token the media has tried to use every tiny detail in this case to try and interject race into the George Zimmerman case when I can hardly imagine a case that had less to do with race in terms of the facts of the case. Even the fact that George Zimmerman lived in a "gated community" they tried to make it seem that he wanted to live in a place where blacks were kept out. Of course the fact that the community is over 20% black (while the general population is only roughly 13% African-American) should immediately squash this fabricated implication. The fact that the media was trying to use this detail against him shows how desperate they were to make a racial connection to the shooting.

The reality is that George Zimmerman was raised in a multi-racial household, dated black women, and even went out of his way to campaign against police brutality against black victims. On January 8th, 2011 just months before the shooting George Zimmerman is recorded making scathing comments against the Sanford Police department. Zimmerman had been angered by the Sanford Police department's reluctance to charge the son of a white police lieutenant who had beaten a black homeless man, namely Sherman Ware. In the September that preceded the shooting Zimmerman wrote an email to Sanford Police Chief Bill Lee saying *"In the past, I have not had a positive perspective of Sanford Police Department,* ***due primarily to the Sherman Ware*** *incident."*

He made it his personal mission to have the Sherman Ware cover-up reviewed which it eventually was and Mr. Ware was able to get some justice, if somewhat delayed.

Take an honest moment and ask yourself this question: have you ever done as much for someone you didn't know personally? Most of you have not. That doesn't make you a racist but let's ask a different question. Try and imagine for a moment that you have strong racist feelings against a particular race. I'm sure you've seen dozens of movie depicting evil racists in movies about the 1950's or any period earlier in Americas history. Imagine you are one of those racists, try and actually think of one of those characters or an openly racist person you have met in your life (I'm sure you've met at least one). Okay so you are that person. Now ask yourself: if the son of a cop went and beat up some homeless person of that race are you going to take time away from your leisure time to go and campaign for that man to receive justice? The obvious answer is that you are not going to do so. Also, are you going to take a member of that race to your prom as your date? Again, the answer is a clear no. Are you going to take your free time and help someone from this race or ethnicity that you hate so much with free tutoring? No you are not.

The obvious truth is that Zimmerman is the furthest thing from being a racist. Not only that I think you would have a hard time finding someone with more evidence of NOT being racist prior to the shooting. In this case the only group pushing a racist and prejudiced perspective is the government-media complex that has gone to great lengths to inject race into this unfortunate but simple case of self-defense.

So now that we have compared and contrasted George Zimmerman with his racial counterpart Roderick Scott in every way we can think of what about the two Martins? Or should I say…

# **GEORGE ZIMMERMAN**: TRAYVON MARTIN, THE BLACK CERVINI

Now that we have compared the shooters in both cases, what about the deceased? Do Trayvon Marin and Christopher Cervini share any important commonalities or is the character of these two teenage men as different as their appearances?

Well just to recap, remember that Christopher Cervini used illicit drugs (he died with marijuana in his system), engaged in underage drinking and smoking (when he died he was intoxicated from drinking at the house of one of his cohorts earlier that night), and was at least a petty thief[41] according to the testimony of his friends that were present the night he was shot. Remember his friends had testified that they and Christopher Cervini had been breaking into cars looking for cigarettes to steal the night of that shooting. Also, if you piece all the testimony together with the police reports about the position of the body it becomes obvious that Cervini was charging at Roderick Scott prior to being shot in self-defense.

---

[41] When it comes to classifying criminal activity in most jurisdictions a theft is considered "petty" if what was stolen amounts to less than $1,000.00; otherwise the theft is considered "grand" as in at least amounting to a grand. This is why most car thefts are referred to as "grand theft autos" because most cars are worth more than a grand.

Prior to the Zimmerman shooting, Trayvon Martin had recently gotten high on marijuana (according to the autopsy report the THC levels indicate within just hours before the shooting). After the shooting, when police arrived, Zimmerman had physical signs of having been severely beaten and conversely a later autopsy would confirm that Martin did not have any similar bruising other than the single gunshot. So prior to the self-defense shooting Zimmerman was being beaten and Trayvon Martin was not. This was not a "fight" but a beating, one that might have been fatal had Zimmerman not been able to defend himself with his firearm.

Well, again we have to acknowledge that no two cases can be considered an exact match; there will always be differences when comparing cases with varying degrees of significance. So, certain aspects in the Martin case are even more clear-cut than in the Cervini case and vice versa. For example, in the Trayvon Martin case it was abundantly obvious that Zimmerman's person was threatened because he had sustained serious injuries and there was **an eyewitness to Zimmerman being beaten**. In the Cervini case, what occurred that night was not as apparent to the arriving police officers that handled that particular case.

On the other hand, what was much more clearly established in the Cervini shooting was that the deceased was absolutely engaged in criminal activity when Roderick Scott approached him that night. In the Zimmerman case there is less concrete evidence to support the claim that George Zimmerman had reason to believe Trayvon was engaged in criminal activity. Even by Mr. Zimmerman's own account he states that it *seemed* to him that Trayvon was "casing out" one of his neighbor's homes while in Roderick's case he could plainly hear and then see that the three teens involved were attempting to break into cars on his street.

Of course this is ultimately an irrelevant detail in both cases since as we have covered **approaching someone on a public street is simply not a crime** or a legally significant event. Until a threat is made, a solicitation to engage in criminal activity is given or the interaction becomes physical does the law start to have a say about **one person simply approaching and questioning another person on the street**. So here we see that the specific details of the cases differ significantly but they are quite similar in most areas of legal significance.

When Cervini charged at Roderick Scott (who had not violated any law up until this point) it then became legal for Mr. Scott to use force to defend himself, plain and simple. The fact that Cervini was not armed is not relevant (especially considering the fact that in the dark of night Scott would have no way of knowing that and besides Cervini could have gained control of Mr. Scott's gun had the shooter not acted). The fact that he was a teenage man was irrelevant. Sure he had "his whole life ahead of him" which he obviously did not value enough to keep him from engaging in criminal activity in the middle of the night making this fact irrelevant.

Excuse me while I muse for a moment but I find some of these expressions that we use to be a little strange. Only a new born baby has their "whole life" ahead of them. After that the rest of us have some smaller fraction thereof ahead of us. I bring this up because sometimes when a self-defense shooting results in the death of an underage criminal this type of language makes it very difficult for the innocent self-defense shooter to get fair treatment, in court but even more so in the media. The fact is that Roderick Scott also had most of his life ahead of him; the same could be said about George Zimmerman who was only in his twenties at the time of the shooting. Because the fallen attacker was a few years younger *(and had admittedly endearing* ***school photos taken five years before the shooting*** *that the media deceptively placed against current pictures of Zimmerman)* we are all supposed to ruin the innocent life of the shooter to balance some sick equivocating scales of injustice?

Of course it is a tragedy when a young person dies in this manner. In my opinion it is even more of a tragedy when their own actions are to blame for their life being cut short because all men must face their creator, but I digress. That said it would also have been a tragedy if Roderick Scott had allowed Christopher Cervini to rush him and get a hold of his handgun and this resulted in Mr. Scott's own demise or the injury of an innocent bystander (or even one of the other two teenagers that did not react to Roderick's approach by trying to attack him as did Christopher).

According to Zimmerman, prior to the shooting his holstered gun became visible to Trayvon Martin who yelled out "YOU ARE GONNA DIE TONIGHT MOTHERF***ER" as he was reaching for Zimmerman's gun to follow through on his violent promise. It was at this point that George Zimmerman grabbed his gun and fired a single shot in self-defense. When Cervini decided to charge at him, Roderick

Scott did not know if he was going to suffer the same fate. Advocates against gun ownership often quote statistics (of questionable veracity don't get me wrong) that suggest that a gun you own is more likely to be used against yourself than an intruder. The numbers they use to make up these numbers are partially from suicides, partially from domestic incidents but are also fed by the fact that a criminal will use any nearby weapon (including your own) to accomplish their goal.

Now that we have established the similarities between Trayvon Martin and Christopher Cervini (including their drug use, criminal behavior and the fact that they both were attacking their shooters) let's put the Roderick Scott case aside and delve a little deeper into what type of individual Trayvon Martin really was. Not all of these details will be legally relevant but you may find it interesting. Also, if you are reading this book as an open-minded member of the Martin camp (which is apparently a distinction in-and-of-itself) try and give me a little slack as I bring up some of these uncomfortable facts. You may feel as you read the next section that "isn't it bad enough that Trayvon had to lose his life now this author has to drag his name through the mud". What I will say to that is that Zimmerman is alive but his name has been dragged through the mud. He has been branded a racist and racial profiler when there is **absolutely no evidence to support** this claim. We have already discussed how destructive to the living it can be when we cripple justice by sticking to a "don't speak ill of the dead" attitude.

That said who was this "boy" that assaulted and battered George Zimmerman, a shorter man in his late twenties?

## Young Man, Drug Dealer, Thief and Violent Attacker

I like to start with a bold statement and then back it up piece by piece (if you haven't noticed by now), so let's start with **the young part**. He was 17 at the time that he attacked George Zimmerman, which is a fact that is not in question. Now I personally do not consider 17 to be particularly young – especially in the context of a physical altercation because many people have been beaten to death by teenage men and so this was a legitimate threat. At 17 years of age I was living abroad and running a professional services group in London and I was certainly responsible for my own actions and decisions, but that is the subject for another book (in fact after this volume is published I will be working on a title called **"Six Figure Teen"** so look for that in 2014). Now had Trayvon really been the 11 year old boy in the pictures that the mainstream media plastered all over the airways (and that the anti-gun bloggers spread throughout the internet) that might be another story. In Jewish culture they consider a boy to become a man when he is 13 years old and has embraced the values of his upbringing. Of course this is a tradition that was established before the Industrial Revolution created a separation of father and son creating the need for perpetual formalized education even for those not pursuing specialized fields. In fact my paternal grandfather was raised Jewish and at the age of 13 (because of unfortunate circumstances) he had to leave school and start working to support the family. He started working in the Garment District running around filling orders for buttons and such until he formed his own garment company years later. He lived a full and rich life and he wasn't deprived because he did wait until his late twenties to stop playing Guitar Hero and start working.

That said our society has been following a steady trend over the past 80 years or so of considering older and older men as children or at least as adolescents *(a term that goes as far back as 1482 and originally referred to the period between puberty and when the teenager could be considered grown and had reached an adult's height).* Adolescence has gone from ending in the middle teenage years to today when psychologists are being given guidelines that state that a man should be considered an adolescent until the ripe age of 25 years old. Take a moment and reflect on the fact that in most civilizations, especially in traditional economies prior to the industrial revolution, someone that has reached 25 years of age has usually had over a decade of experience in their trade or field of expertise, is likely married and has started their own family already. My point is simply that when a full grown six foot tall teenage man attacks a concerned neighbor that is simply questioning them about what they are up to on their street at night we have to stop treating these cases like the attacker is some innocent child simply because they have not yet reached 20 years old and their victim was an older man that was able to defend themselves (and yes I am referring to Zimmerman as a victim – if a third party had stepped in to defend him he would be enjoying a unanimous chorus of sympathy for being so badly beaten just for being a concerned neighbor).

Put another way, we need to at least teach our children that if they are going to attack an older man on the street, in the dark, ***make sure they aren't armed before you decide to start attacking them***. They need to know that, unlike some defenseless kid that happens to be attending their high school, many men are able to defend themselves when they are attacked, as they are legally and ethically able to do in good conscience. There are not many justified uses of force but the one use of force that is almost universally accepted is when it is done in self-defense.

So, indeed Trayvon Martin was a young man for sure. It is also true that his death was an unfortunate tragedy. It's a shame that he didn't learn from his parents, his multiple step-mothers, the two households which he bounced back and forth from when his parents split up, from school and from society in general not to use drugs, get in fights and bang the heads of armed community watchmen against hard pavement. Again, I am not referencing his upbringing to water down his own culpability that night, not at all. I am just trying to make a point that these parents should be ashamed of their fallen child not leading the campaign to have him sainted.

Now as far as I am concerned Trayvon Martin was a grown man making his own decisions that night, but if it were my child I would be questioning myself to see what I could have done differently in raising him. I would be apologizing to the community for having a child that was using and dealing drugs to their children, engaging in illegal arms deals *(although if the 2nd amendment was still in effect would there really be such a thing as an illegal arms purchase?)*, and that was **acting out on his thirst for violence** in school and on the street. Let's back up some of these claims that I've been throwing around before I lose you.

### Trayvon, the Illicit Apothecary

These pictures were **not shown** by the prosecution and the mainstream media after the Trayvon Martin murder while America was forming its opinion of the case:

***Figure 20**: Disturbing Photos Taken From Trayvon's Cell Phone*

Here are some pictures of Trayvon in the act of smoking (which from how he is smoking and the look of the smoke it is most likely marijuana smoke):

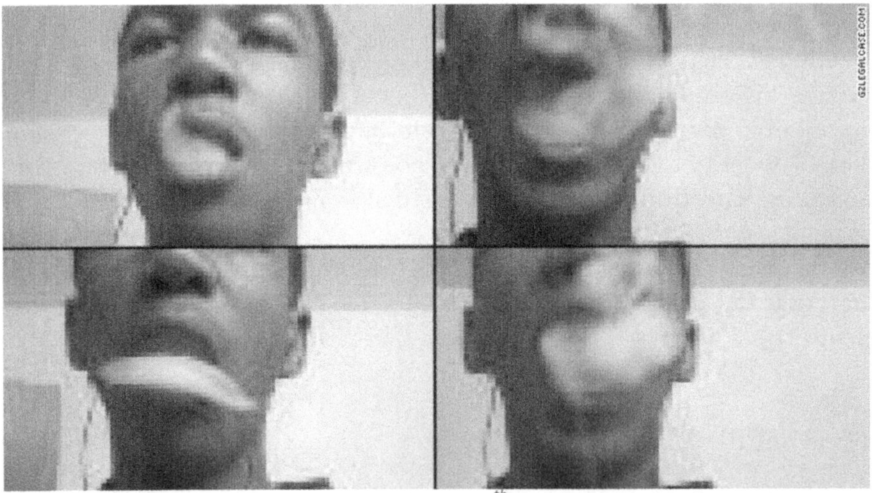


***Figure 21**: Photos More Recent Than His 5$^{th}$ Grade Wallet Sized Portraits*

Well, the pictures to some extent speak for themselves: obviously Trayvon was a drug user. The autopsy report confirmed as much but it is always helpful to have pictures. Now the **picture of the gun and the**

**marijuana plant** suggest more than just drug use and are consistent with someone growing and/or dealing drugs. Is there anything besides the pictures to suggest this?

Well, on February 5th the following was retrieved from Martin's Facebook page under the screen name "Trayvon Slimm Martin":

> *DumbRyte – "Yeoo happy birthday ! but pik up the fone or hmu*[42] ***we got business to talk!***"
>
> *Slimm – "NO PHON"*
>
> *DumbRyte -- "damn were u at a nigga* **need a plant.**" *(Emphasis Ours)*

Now it is obvious that "DumbRyte" is making reference to marijuana when he laments that he needs 'a plant' unless Martin was engaged in the rare orchid trade with fellow grammatically challenged horticulture enthusiasts through his Facebook page (however that seems like the less plausible explanation). Also he refers to this future transaction as "business" to Trayvon which fits if he dealt drugs (and this fits with the pictures of marijuana plants).

That said, if you throw a rock into any random high school and hit a student there is a one in four chance that they use marijuana (the numbers are much higher in the "has ever used" category, this is current/recent use[43] I'm talking about) so the fact that Trayvon Martin was a pot head is not altogether that significant (it really only becomes necessary to mention to thwart the unreality created by the media with their clever use of photos from when he was 11 and edited 911 tapes).

---

[42] HMU is text slang for "hit me up" meaning to 'follow up with me'.

[43] I have an ebook being released shortly called "Zombie Thinkers: The Dumbfication of Emuriqa" that will dig a little deeper into the issue of legal and illegal drug use in this country.

Did Martin use or manufacture any other forms of drugs, besides marijuana? Well, interestingly enough here is a discussion regarding a drug that I had never heard of prior to this case called Lean (the first part is about Codeine):

***Figure 22**: Trayvon Seeking Codeine*

So Trayvon was seeking to obtain liquid Codeine, but why? In the next interchange we learn that he is looking for the liquid version of Codeine to make a narcotic drink known as Lean:

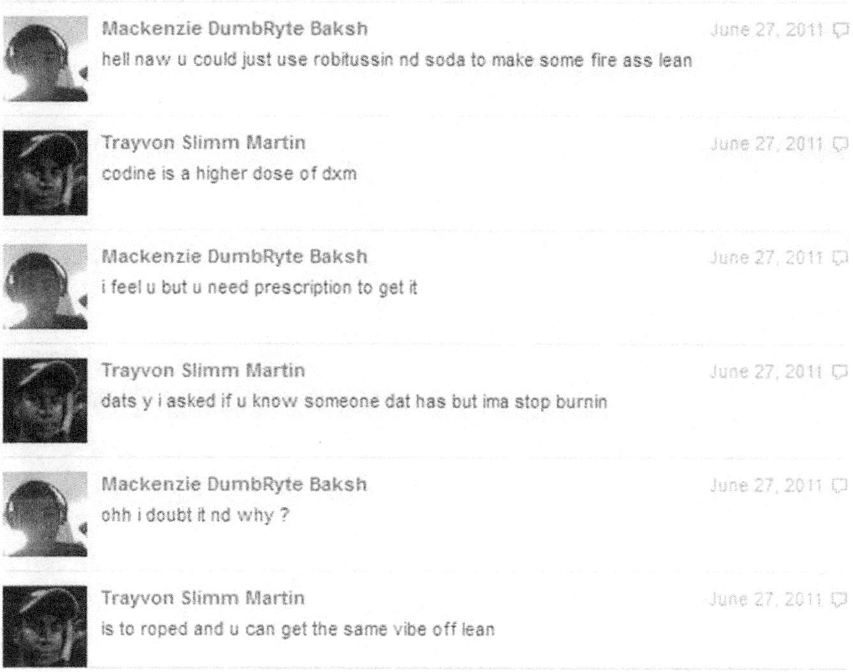


***Figure 23****: Trayvon Seeks to Make Lean*

We all have heard at nausea that Trayvon Martin was innocently returning from the store with candy and iced tea. Being a lover of iced tea myself when I heard this I was curious about what type of iced tea he had purchased and found that detail hard to attain at first. Then I heard someone say he had "Arizona Iced Tea" but I was still curious about what flavor. Then I come to find out that he had purchased "Arizona Watermelon Fruit Juice Cocktail" and not iced tea that night along with Skittles. At this point I just chalked this up to liberal political-correction laden reporters being too scared to come off like they were exploiting a stereo type and preferring a comfortable euphemistic lie. No big deal, it didn't really matter; I was simply curious about what he was getting that night.

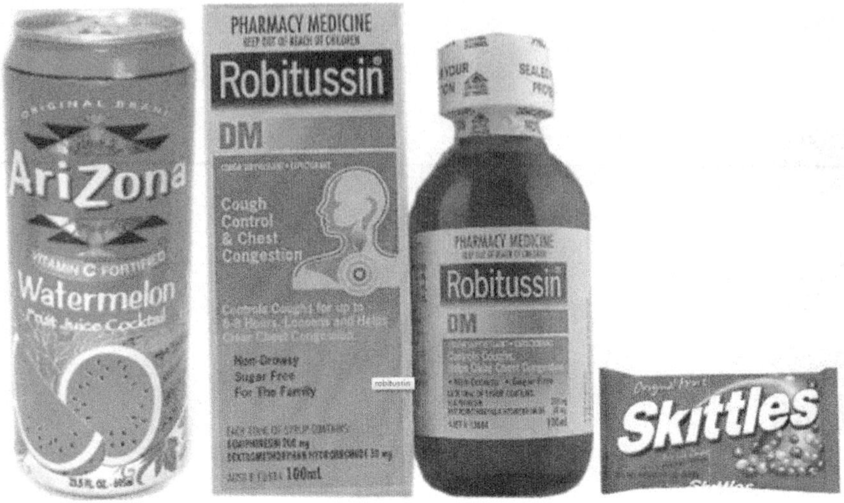


*Figure 24: Recipe for Lean*

Then I find out that this drink (or Sprite) can be used in making a narcotic drink called Lean as mentioned above. Well, surely this is just a meaningless coincidence. Then I find out that another important ingredient is either Jolly Ranchers or Skittles… wait, weren't there a bunch of protesters holding up bags of Skittles for some confounding reason? That's right along with his watermelon fruit juice he picked up Skittles. So let's catch up a bit. That night he: **was already high** on marijuana, he goes out to get **two out of three ingredients to make Lean** and we have a documented online conversation about Trayvon Martin's **preference to make and use Lean** as his narcotic of choice. Now this stops being a meaningless detail.

I always say there is a difference between what you can prove and what is reasonable to believe. No one can prove that Trayvon Martin bought that specific drink and candy to make Lean the night he perished, however I certainly believe that to be the case. Remember, he walked a mile in the rain to get a single can of juice and some candy and certainly if they had some greater purpose it would help to explain this. Again, please don't take this to mean that drug users (or even drug dealers) should all be shot. However, when people seek to turn a fallen attacker into a saint and use misleading photos and labels then this type of information needs to be brought forward.

So with the available evidence it is reasonable to believe that Trayvon Martin used and sold (and likely grew) marijuana and that he made and used Lean. I don't want to get too deep into the details on Lean but you should know that this make-shift drug (with its active component known as "DXM") is associated with many of the **paranoid and violence-inducing effects** that are commonly associated with PCP and similar drugs. We will explore Trayvon's recent history with violence a little later but this is certainly an interesting detail since we know that he reacted violently to Zimmerman's inquiries.

## Trayvon the Thief

It is without pleasure that I report this all to you. I wish none of these things were true about Trayvon or any other young person today. However, it is not my fault that **they are true** and in the event that I have misstated something I invite you to continue this dialogue and send me a rational and reasoned explanation of your point and if something needs to be corrected I will do so and release an updated edition of this volume (nilesmercado@gmail.com).

So before getting into Trayvon's violent past leading up to the shooting let's focus on if there is any evidence that he was a thief. Remember that Zimmerman claimed that Trayvon was ***casing out a residential location*** and he approached him out of his legitimate concern that there had been multiple robberies in his multicultural neighborhood (remember this was not a "white gated community" as originally reported). Now, while there was a corroborating witness to Zimmerman being brutalized by Martin only George Zimmerman himself witnessed Trayvon casing out the house in question. This would be much simpler if (as in the Roderick Scott case) there were witnesses to this ancillary criminal behavior. That said, we have no particular reason to doubt George Zimmerman's account that has been consistent from day one and otherwise fits with the other facts available in this case. But is the idea of Trayvon Martin casing out a location for a robbery consistent with his recent past or his character in general?

Well, we've already covered that he was a drug user and drug dealer and there is certainly a lot of overlap with those activities and other criminal behavior. But then again there are a lot of drug users that have never gone so far as to rob a stranger's home. Well, you may or may not be aware that Trayvon Martin was found at school with a backpack filled with stolen jewelry and some sort of flat headed "burglary tool" as it was referred to in the schools report. Chances are good that you don't know the whole story so here it is.

Ironically, if it was not for Frances Robles writing a Miami Herald article on March 26th 2012 an entire chain of events would not have taken place.

It was that Robles article, and the outlining of the Miami-Dade School Police Department's report on a Trayvon Martin incident from October 2011, that kicked off an internal investigation by M-DSPD Police Chief Hurley against his own officers to find out who leaked the police report.

*[Note: The **Miami-Dade Public School System has its own Police force**, and Chief, who report to the School Board and Superintendent - Not the Police Dept – but remember **this is still police** and not security guards. The Police Chief is appointed by the School Superintendent, in this example, **Alberto Carvalho**].*

Fullsize — Image 1 of 10 — previous | next

**Related Content**

- Krop classmates arrive at school wearing black to protest Trayvon case

The Miami Gardens teen who has become a national symbol of racial injustice was suspended three times, and had a spotty school record that his family's attorneys say is irrelevant to the facts that led up to his being gunned down on Feb. 26.

2011

In October, a school police investigator said he saw Trayvon on the school surveillance camera in an unauthorized area "hiding and being suspicious." Then he said he saw Trayvon mark up a door with "W.T.F" — an acronym for "what the f— -." The officer said he found Trayvon the next day and went through his book bag in search of the graffiti marker.

Instead the officer reported he found women's jewelry and a screwdriver that he described as a "burglary tool," according to a Miami-Dade Schools Police report obtained by The Miami Herald. Word of the incident came as the family's lawyer acknowledged that the boy was suspended in February for getting caught with an empty bag with traces of marijuana, which he called "irrelevant" and an attempt to demonize a victim.

Trayvon's backpack contained 12 pieces of jewelry, in addition to a watch and a large flathead screwdriver, according to the report, which described silver wedding bands and earrings with diamonds.

Trayvon was asked if the jewelry belonged to his family or a girlfriend.

"Martin replied it's not mine. A friend gave it to me," he responded, according to the report. Trayvon

***Figure 25**: Martin Found with Stolen Jewelry and Watch at School*

If the type is too small to read the important thing to understand is that it was actually that M-DSPD internal affairs investigation which revealed in October 2011 Trayvon Martin was searched by School Resource Officer, **Darryl Dunn**. The search of Trayvon Martin's backpack turned up at least 12 pieces of ladies jewelry, and a man's watch, in addition to a flat head screwdriver described as "a burglary tool".

When Trayvon was questioned about who owned the jewelry and where it came from, he claimed he was just holding it for a "friend". A "friend" he would not name.

Later, after the police report was outlined in the Robles article, and despite Trayvon being suspended for the second time in a new school year, Martin family attorney, Benjamin Crump, said Trayvon's dad, Tracy Martin, and Trayvon's mom, Sybrina Fulton, did not know anything about the jewelry case. It was only as a consequence of the M-DSPD internal affairs investigation that "why" they may not have known came to light.

Not to be defensive but when I bring up the following information keep in mind that I am just presenting to you the facts I have available. I leave it to you to make the inferences or connections you choose to make. That said, what I find interesting is that on **October 21st 2011** a **burglary took place a few blocks from** Krop Senior High School where Trayvon Martin attended. The stolen property outlined in the Miami-Dade Police Report (PD111021-422483) **matches the description presented by SRO Dunn** in his School Police report 2011-11477.

Notice the following map showing the proximity to the robbery containing the matching loot found in Trayvon Martin's backpack to the school where Martin attended:

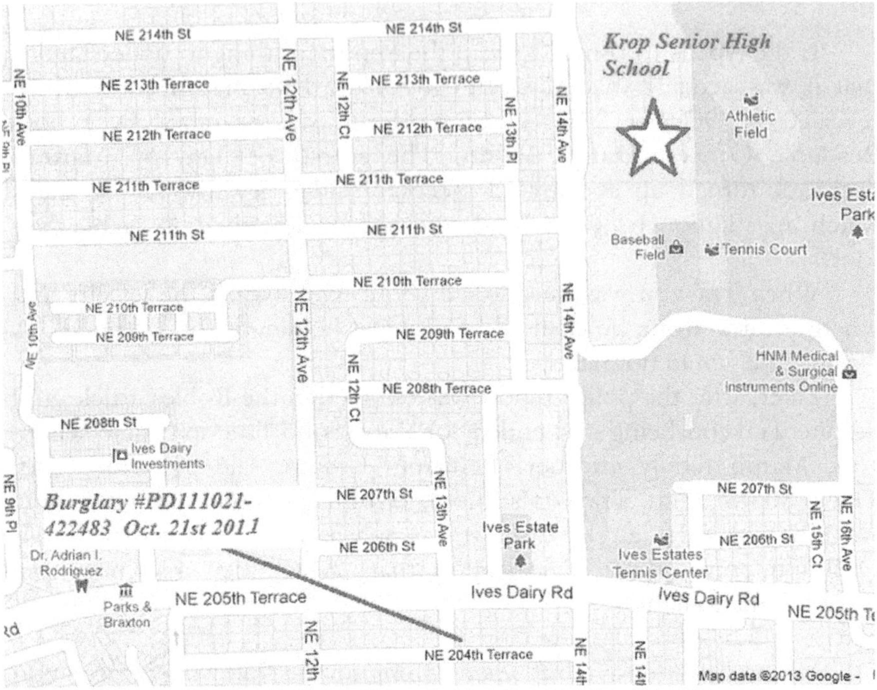


*Figure 26: Nearby Stolen Property Matches Martin's School Report*

However, there was **one big issue** preventing these two reports from being officially linked. SRO Dunn never filed a **criminal** report, nor opened a **criminal** investigation, surrounding the stolen jewelry. Instead, and as a result of pressure from M-DSPD Chief Hurley to avoid criminal reports for black male students, **Dunn wrote up the jewelry as "found items"**, and transferred them, along with the burglary tool, to the Miami-Dade Police property room where they sat on a shelf unassigned to anyone for investigation.

A separate report of "criminal Mischief" (T-08809) was filed for the additional issue of writing "WTF" on a school locker. (It was the search for the marker used to write the graffiti that led to the backpack search).

The school discipline, "suspension", was **attached to the graffiti and not the stolen jewelry**.

Tagle AFFIDAVIT pAGES 49-5

Q. ...

A. In reference to the found property, because he told me he wrote it up as "found property" because of the situation, that there was a lot of arrests being made at Michael Krop; there were a lot of drug-related cases and they needed to cut back on any type of crime that was going on there, and that it came up from his supervisor up the chain.

... a little bit

*Figure 27: Stolen Jewelry Marked as "Found Property"*

The connections between the Police Burglary report and the School Report of "found items" were never made because the regular police detective in charge of the Burglary case had no idea the School Police Dept. had filed a "found items" report.

Two differing police departments, and the School Officer, Dunn, intentionally took the criminal element out of the equation – instead preferring "school discipline" and not "criminal adjudication".

It was only when the M-DSPD Internal Affairs investigation kicked in, and six officers gave sworn affidavits, that this manipulative scheme to improve criminal statistics within the School System came to light.

School Superintendent Alberto Carvalho gave his hire, Police Chief Hurley, instructions to reduce the criminal behavior of young black males. The chosen strategy between them, to ensure optical success, was to stop using the Criminal Justice System to punish black student behavior. Instead they instructed the School Resource Officers to **use school discipline in place of criminal justice** to improve the numbers. This is the type of false accomplishments that get pushed in American schools (especially those that are failing more than most) that keep any real progress from being made.

Another approach was the use of The Baker Act, to quantify behaviors under health HIPPA law secrecy by assigning the students with psychological problems. This allowed them to again use school discipline and work around criminal reports.

**Without the reports, the statistics would improve immensely; and improve they did**. Take a look for yourself:

# Media Advisory

*Miami-Dade County Public Schools*

*Office of Public Relations - 1450 N.E. 2nd Avenue, Miami, FL 33132 - 305-995-1126 - dadeschools.net*

**FOR IMMEDIATE RELEASE**
Wednesday, February 15, 2012

**CONTACT: John Schuster**
Miami-Dade County Public Schools
305-995-1126

**MIAMI-DADE SCHOOLS POLICE REDUCES JUVENILE DELINQUENCY BY 60 PERCENT**

(MIAMI)-Miami-Dade Schools Police (M-DSPD) was recently commended by the Florida Department of Juvenile Justice (DJJ) for dramatically decreasing school-related delinquency in Miami-Dade County public schools.

M-DSPD has the distinction of decreasing school-related juvenile delinquency by an impressive 60 percent for the last six months of 2011, which was the largest decline in any school district in the state. The police force is being heralded for adopting effective alternatives to arrest such as civil citations. The M-DSPD has also seen a 35 percent decrease in the amount of referrals to the DJJ.

"Three years ago we set out to create and maintain a police department focused on redefining our role and reaffirming our values through prevention, intervention, enforcement and education. Our mantra is education not incarceration," said Chief of Schools Police Charles J. Hurley.

M-DSPD has taken a student-centered approach to law enforcement by engaging and helping students and their families. With the assistance of school leadership, involved parents and community stakeholders, the police department has been able to cut student arrests by a remarkable 35 percent.

"I'm extremely proud of our men and women on the police force. It is our intent to demonstrate compassion and understanding to our students and their families when it comes to law enforcement. We have a student-centered police department first and foremost," said Superintendent of Schools Alberto M. Carvalho.

The police department achieved success by employing many strategies including diversion programs, mentoring, policy reform, home visits, truancy sweeps and public support. Through these initiatives, graduation rates and student employability have increased.

# # #

12-JJS/282/DF

Back to News Releases

***Figure 28**: Winner: Statistics, Loser: Reality*

This type of deception didn't end there. The final approach, to ensure no one would find out about the manipulation, was to change the

Standard Operating Procedure (SOP) for inter-agency information sharing.

This new SOP was outlined by a communications directive in 2010 forbidding the sharing of Miami-Dade School Police reports to outside agencies without redaction. Officers had to send any and all requests through the public information officer.

Hence, the furor of Chief Hurley when the Robles article hit the press and cited police reports – **Hurley smelled a leaker and launched an investigation.**

Ultimately the internal affairs investigation initiated by Hurley led to his own firing, because the officers questioned told the internal affairs investigators the truth of what was going on and ousted the scheme.

One of the examples of this in action was the jewelry incident and Trayvon Martin – as accidentally outlined in the Herald report. But the Herald **never knew their reporting had launched an internal affairs investigation** which led to the collapse of the scheme.

Meanwhile the stolen **jewelry from the burglary (PD111021-422483)** was sitting on a shelf in the Property Room **listed as (2011-11477 "found items")** gathering dust.

Until we started digging, and the FOIA requests revealed not only the scheme but the fact that **a victim was never made whole** with the return of their items, **they never even knew their items were being held in a police locker…**

# That is, until now.

Recently **we contacted Detective Manresa**, assigned to the burglary case, of the Miami-Dade Police Department to **notify him that some of his victims' stolen items** were actually in the Miami-Dade property room! Take a look at the letter we sent him:

Subject: **Attn: Detective Omar Manresa [RE: PD111021-422483 Burglary at XXXX XX XXXXX]**

*Dear Detective Manresa,*

*Per phone conversation of 4/30/13 @ 10:20am regarding* ***burglary incident #PD111021-422483***

*During the course of research surrounding an Internal Affairs M-DSPD investigation in March/April of 2012 it coincidentally came to our attention that School Resource Officer Darryl Dunn (Dr. Krop Senior High School) filled out a report of items from a student's backpack without criminal attachment.*

*The internal documentation used by SRO Dunn only listed the contents of the backpack as "found items" and a burglary tool. He was trying to avoid subjecting the student [Trayvon Martin] to a criminal investigation, therefore no criminal report, nor was an investigation initiated.*

*This action by SRO Dunn was taken at the direction and request of former M-DSPD Police Chief Hurley who had advised his officers to* **avoid writing criminal reports on student offenders***; apparently in an attempt to artificially improve the recorded criminal student statistics.*

*The* ***internal report #2011-11477*** *never attached the stolen property to the student who was carrying it when searched. The property was taken to the custody of Carmen Gonzalez, Property Specialist, where it was held, and still should be located.*

*The details surrounding this event are outlined in the following sworn affidavits completed by members of the Miami-Dade School Police Department (they are extensive).*

*http://www.scribd.com/doc/135564937/Sergeant-William-Tagle-Internal-Affairs-Investigative-Report http://www.scribd.com/doc/135684004/Steven-N-Hadley-Sr-affidavit-and-investigation*

*http://www.scribd.com/doc/135692728/Affidavit-From-Commander-Deanna-Fox-Williams*

*http://www.scribd.com/doc/136164820/sergeant-Lourdes-Hodges-Sworn-Statement-Affidavit*

*http://www.scribd.com/doc/136392330/Sworn-affidavit-of-Detective-Gylamar-Ochoa-MDSPD*

*http://www.scribd.com/doc/136642019/Sergeant-Bradley-Rosh-MDSPD-Sworn-Affidavit*

> *As mentioned,* **if you contact the victim of Miami-Dade burglary #PD111021-422483**, *and review with them the property confiscated by M-DSPD SRO Dunn* **listed under #2011-11477**, *we believe you will be able to return at least a portion of the stolen merchandise.*
>
> *Perhaps some of the items returned may have sentimental, as well as obvious financial, value.*
>
> [CLOSING SALUTATIONS REMOVED]

---

It is our genuine hope that this property gets returned to its rightful owners. My wife was once without some jewelry that was given to her by her deceased grandmother with whom she was very close and I know how upsetting that sort of thing can be. Let's hope that politics don't get in the way of normal procedure as they have several times during this case.

We chose not to include all of the above referenced documents in this book because we wanted to keep this book fairly trim so that the most important information could be easily and quickly absorbed. That said we invite you to look at the affidavits and reports for yourself at the link locations that we gave to Detective Omar Manresa.

So now that we have covered the drug use, the apparent drug dealing and the evidence of Trayvon's involvement in at least one case of criminal theft (giving credence to Zimmerman's claim that Trayvon was casing out a house for a robbery the night he approached him), we are compelled to cover perhaps the most disturbing aspect of this young man's past that has oddly gone unnoticed by most media outlets.

## Trayvon the Violent

After all this I don't want to spend too much time on the violent past that Trayvon Martin had since I think you are getting the point by now. Ultimately this information is not proof-positive of anything that occurred the night that Trayvon perished but it does paint an unfortunate picture.

Now, you may have heard that Trayvon Martin was into **Mixed Martial Arts** (MMA) style fighting and was **repeatedly getting into fights at school**. Fighting in school is fairly common, especially with kids that deal drugs and come from broken homes. That isn't what disturbed me when researching for this book. What struck me was an interchange he had with a female friend on November $21^{st}$, 2011 (again just months before the shooting).

This conversation was lifted from a text messaging session on his cell phone and really shows where Martin's head was at leading up to his encounter with George Zimmerman. There is a lot of slang and misspellings so bear with me here. I think the only decoding you will need to know is that "bae" is often text short form of "babe"; also it is not clear who he is talking about fighting. Prior to the following passage he told her that he was tired and sore from a fight and the female friend asked why he had fought.

| | |
|---|---|
| **Martin**: | Cause man that nigga snitched on me |
| Friend: | Why you always fighting man, you got suspended? |
| **Martin**: | Naw we thumped affta school. |
| Friend: | Ohh damee |
| **Martin**: | I lost the first round :( but won the 2nd and third... |
| Friend: | Ohhh so it was 3 rounds? Damn well at least you won lol |

| | |
|---|---|
| | but you needa stop fighting, for real. |
| **Martin**: | Nay Im not doen with fool... he gone hav 2 see me again |
| Friend: | Nooo...stop, you waint gunn bee satisfied till yuh get suspended again huh? |
| **Martin**: | Naw but **he aint bleed nuff 4 me, only his nose**[44]. *(emphasis ours)* |

So, some of the circumstances are unclear. Particularly unclear is if this was some sort of consensual Fight Club type fighting that they were both engaging in that actually had semi-official "rounds" of fighting or if he is simply talking about some kid he fought with one afternoon wherein their fight simply got interrupted twice (which he then chose to use to characterize the fighting as being in three distinct rounds).

What should be extremely clear from this is that Trayvon Martin was **not some "gentle soul"** as he has been characterized in the media. Rather he was a violent and seemingly disturbed young man. His **thirst for violence is really on show** in the above text conversation when he says (when translated into English) that he isn't done with the fool he fought and the reason being that he **'didn't bleed enough'** for Trayvon to be satisfied.

Since we weren't present during his encounter with George Zimmerman we can't be completely sure what was said in their conversation prior to Trayvon Martin getting violent with Mr. Zimmerman. What should be obvious is that it likely **would not have taken much** for Trayvon to become violent. This is why comparisons of Trayvon Martin to the **innocent Emmett Till** are so absurd and insulting to the memory of Mr. Till. At the time that Emmett was attacked he had not exhibited any violence toward his racist attackers. Conversely, we know from Martin's autopsy that before George Zimmerman fired the single shot in self-defense that he had not been at all violent toward Trayvon Martin (at least not in any way that could be medically observed post-mortem). On the other hand **the evidence**

[44] Some reports of this text message says "aint breed nuff" but even if that was the actual text it is clear from the context that he is not referring to his opponent not having enough children and the reference to his nose makes it clear that he is talking about bleeding and not breeding.

**was all over Zimmerman's person that Martin had injured him severely**: drawing blood, bruising his eyes, and breaking his nose among other injury.

Had George Zimmerman not tried to defend himself how far would Trayvon Martin have gone that night? We know three rounds of fighting with his unknown opponent at school wasn't enough for Martin because his classmate didn't **'bleed nuff' to satisfy Martin's blood lust**. How much would George Zimmerman have had to bleed that night for him to be satisfied?

Stepping out of the realm of what can be positively proved in a court of law I can say that it is my belief that Martin would not have stopped until he delivered on his threat that night. Remember that Zimmerman in his police report recounted Martin's threat as:

**"You're gonna die tonight** mother f***er".

Those are chilling words from a man with a documented **blood lust**. I say "documented" because although these texts were not admissible in court – because the possibility is always there with texting that someone else *could have* sent the texts – you know that the texts from his phone are from him. There is no reason for anyone else to be using his phone to talk to his female schoolmate. In real life the owner of the phone is the one that sends texts from it. When other people are using someone else's phone to text someone there is usually a comment to that affect *"This is Niles, so-and-so is in the shower..."* if you know what I mean and that was not the case in the above text session.

# CONCLUSION

Yes it was a tragedy that Trayvon Martin had to die on the night he was approached by George Zimmerman. This was a tragedy that could have been prevented had he simply not attacked him. Had he not responded to a non-violent inquiry with violence he would likely be alive today. You know as well as I do that he didn't die because of racism. I'm not saying that racism doesn't exist, but there is no evidence of there being even a single racist bone in Zimmerman's body. Beyond that we have positive evidence supporting the fact that Zimmerman was not racist and actual evidence that he cared about African-American individuals. He dated black women, tutored black students for free, grew up in a household with black 'family' members and he had a black business partner. Beyond that he campaigned for justice for a black homeless man that was beaten by the son of a white police officer.

You know that this man didn't harbor any hatred toward black people. The very thought is absurd and insulting to our intelligence. This was not a man that judged people by their skin color but by the "content of their character". Of course today we know a lot more about the content of Trayvon Martin's character and for the most part it paints a very lamentable story.

As a side note, all this discussion about "judging someone based on the content of their character" is obviously referencing Dr. Martin Luther King Jr. and his criteria of what it would mean to live in a world without racism. Interestingly, **the niece** of the late civil rights leader, namely **Dr. Alveda King**, has spoken out to defend the verdict in the Zimmerman case: "**There was reasonable doubt in that case**... so the case went the ways of the laws of this land."

So she agreed with the verdict in the Zimmerman case and had the guts to go on the record saying as much. Going a step further she has been critical of the race baiters in the mainstream media: "As far as trying to **pit the Caucasians against African-Americans**... we are one blood, one human family, one human race, there's a lot of **deception and emotion** in these things **that are being spurred**".

What I find most interesting about her public comments is her reaction to a photo depicting MLK wearing a hoodie suggesting that he would be rallying behind the Trayvon Martin protests if he were alive today: "I can almost promise you **Dr. Martin Luther King, Jr. would not wear a hoodie**" (emphasis ours)

All George Zimmerman knew at first about Trayvon's character is that it appeared to him that Martin was casing out a house for a future robbery. If Zimmerman was correct or incorrect in that assessment is unknown and irrelevant. What Zimmerman knew for sure after encountering Trayvon is that this teenage man had threatened to kill him and that he was half way toward living up to the threat when he shot him in self-defense.

If you believe that Zimmerman would have just lied there and let a white person beat him to death then you must have a **mental deficiency**. If you state that he would not have stopped a white teenager that appeared to be casing out one of his neighbor's houses then you must have some magical ability to concoct conclusions out of zero evidence because there is **absolutely no evidence** to support this and tons of evidence to counter this claim.

Also, if you do not believe that Trayvon Martin was beating up George Zimmerman that night then you have to believe a lot of goofy things to make that absurd assertion fit the facts. You have to believe that the only eyewitness (besides Zimmerman) made up their testimony just for the thrill of misleading a jury against fear of being charged with perjury. You have to believe that Zimmerman injured himself or that there was some mysterious "second hitter" that brutalized him and then fled the scene without being noticed by anyone including Zimmerman.

If you believe that this was a "fight" and not just a case of Zimmerman being beaten by Martin (as Martin had beat his classmate earlier) then you have to explain why an autopsy could not find any indication of Trayvon Martin sustaining any bruises or injury prior to being shot.

Of course, the reality is that if you are still reading my book at this point you likely agree to a large degree with my findings. I don't say that because of how compellingly I was able to present the information in this volume *(although I hope I have done well on that front)* but rather I say this because **people seeking to saint** Trayvon Martin and demonize George Zimmerman are for the most part **not that interested in the facts** of this case. In general they are more interested in pushing the racial narrative being super-imposed onto this case.

If not that then they are usually so vehemently against the idea of **personal gun ownership** that it just bothers them that someone used a firearm to defend themselves. Many people are clamoring for tighter gun laws so that gun ownership laws in this country can more closely reflect those that existed under Mao Tse-tung, Hitler, Pol Pot and Stalin. You may agree with that type of gun control which is really a totally separate subject. I only bring it up again here because it has certainly shaped people's perception along with the misinformation from the mainstream media, the efforts of the persecution (oh I mean prosecution – sorry) to hide the truth at every turn and by peoples own prejudice against whites that choose to arm themselves.

The discussion is far from over. I want to hear from you and continue this dialogue. Even if you disagree completely with me, even now, and you are one of those rare Martin supporters that is open to reasonable and logical dialogue I still want to hear from you. I am a firm believer that **you can learn a lot from people that disagree with you** and see things from a completely different perspective.

Above all I hope that **you are never put in the situation that George Zimmerman or Roderick Scott were in** the nights they felt compelled to approach criminals on their street and then had to face not only an attacker but an out-of-control prosecutorial machine that tried to turn them into career making cases.

Also, I hope that you are **never put in the position that O.J. Simpson was put in**, namely being put in the unenviable position of being accused of a crime that you had no part in committing.

Hopefully you will never be put in those positions. Also, if I have been successful with this small book I have written then maybe you will be **a little more suspicious and a little more sympathetic** the next time one of your fellow citizens is being targeted by the state. For we are all at risk of being the next target each and every time,

# When Prosecutors Attack!

# INDEX

I hope you enjoy the index that follows. In addition to being useful I've tried to include any fun references that are made throughout the body of the text. Enjoy!

## 9



## A



## B



## C



## D

## E



## F



## G



## J



## K

## L



## M



## N



## O



## P



## R

## S



## T



## W

# ABOUT THE AUTHOR

**Niles Mercado** has about two decades of experience consulting for various government agencies including the Air Force and the Department of Justice. He resides in America's beautiful southwest with his amazingly supportive wife and precious daughter. To maintain his privacy and his family's safety he has chosen to write this volume using the pen name "Niles Mercado"; in light of the recent murders of several Zimmermann supporters *(and the fact that one of his researchers had their* ***car set on fire in a police parking lot****)* can you really blame him?

He is sincere when he invites his readers to contact him about his writing and continue the dialogue. Niles is currently working on several projects so feedback about his current books, other prosecutorial misconduct, governmental abuses and other related topics are especially welcome!

nilesmercado@gmail.com
Twitter: @CorruptionShow

# NOTES

Made in the USA
Monee, IL
05 November 2026

67377198R00111